THE BRAIN GAME

This type of question measures your vocabulary skills and the range of your verbal flexibility.
A. You adapt or *set* lyrics to music.
B. You state or *tell* your position.
C. A bank teller counts or *tells* the money.
E. You arrange or *set* up a time.
The word "copy" is not a synonym to either. The answer is "D."

Tests 7, 14, 15, and 19 measure verbal skills.

If you have strong problem solving abilities, then this question was probably easy for you.

The first two numbers in any row vertically or horizontally are multiplied. The third number is the quotient. Therefore, the correct answer is "1."

Tests 2 and 5 measure arithmetic aptitude skills.

In order to solve this problem, you must fold up the patterns mentally to see which three dimensional object results. In this instance, the correct answer is "B." (Although "A" looks the most obviously correct, it actually does not fold into a box.)

The visualization skills required to answer questions like this correctly are measured in Tests 11 and 12.

A strong ability to analyze a sequence and ascertain the rules that govern it is required to answer this question correctly. The line and the square have a fixed relationship, but they move in the box counterclockwise: first one side at a time, then they skip a side, then skip two sides. To achieve the correct answer, the line and square must skip three sides. The answer is "A."

Analytical skills are also examined in Test 13.

To solve this problem, you must combine your ability to visualize in three dimensions and count accurately. If you counted 32 blocks, then you answered correctly.

Test 16 measures this ability.

This question requires a strong ability to analyze a problem and break it down into its various components. "Q" is represented by the small circle and "S" by the horizontal line. Therefore, the answer is "B."

Similar skills are examined in Tests 2 and 13.

Perhaps its true that aesthetics are a matter of personal taste, but our sources say that good taste follows certain visual rules. The vase judged most aesthetic is the one on the right.

Creative skills and aesthetic judgment are measured in Tests 8, 10, and 12.

This question is quite difficult and requires a creative approach. To answer correctly, you are required to recognize various parts of the figures and move them around in your mind. All of the figures contain the letter "z" except for figure "B" in which the "z" is written backwards. The answer is "B."

Figure recognition is measured in Tests 24 and 27, while creative associations are examined in Tests 9 and 10.

The ability to solve problems in logic is considered by psychologists to be an indicator of intellectual maturity. Although statements "C" and "D" could be true by themselves, they are not supported by the original premise. In fact, none of the statements is supported. Therefore, the correct answer is "E."

Logic and comprehension skills are measured in Tests 3, 4, and 17.

THE BRAIN GAME

Rita Aero and Elliot Weiner, Ph.D.

QUILL

New York, 1983

ACKNOWLEDGMENTS

Our thanks go to Susan Whitney, Barbara Stewart, Ph.D., and George Csicsery, M.A., for their help with the test norming research. We also wish to convey our appreciation to the psychologists and researchers who have generously allowed us to share their tests with our readers. We are indebted to Stephanie Rick for her help with the book's design and to Scott Bartlett for many of the illustrations on the cover and throughout. Finally, we are grateful to James Landis, our editor, for his encouragement and support of this project — and to Natalie, Neal, and B.J. for their love and understanding.

Library of Congress Catalog Card Number: 83-61196

ISBN: 0-688-01923-4

Printed in the United States of America

6 7 8 9 10

CONTENTS

HOW TO USE THIS BOOK

The Brain Game consists of a series of 27 aptitude tests divided into several categories. The first test you will take, the IQ Test, will explore and measure the breadth of your creative and intellectual abilities and will examine your skill in test taking. Once you have found your IQ (intelligence quotient) with this test, you can go on to the four chapters that follow to pinpoint your special abilities.

Chapter One explores the skills of your left brain — that hemisphere of the brain which excels in linear logic. This chapter includes tests of verbal skills, mathematics, formal logic and analysis, and scientific knowledge.

Chapter Two looks at your right-brain abilities. The right hemisphere of the brain specializes in visual and spatial understanding and in creative, intuitive knowing. Those who are right-brained will do especially well on these tests, which measure aesthetic judgment, spatial orientation, visual analysis, and creative imagination.

Chapter Three examines the functioning of your software — the programming that allows your mind to synthesize and combine the diverse abilities of both hemispheres. The tests in this chapter explore your aptitude for abstract reasoning, visual analysis, discerning word meanings, and reading comprehension.

Chapter Four measures your hardware abilities. The hardware is the neurophysiological circuitry of the brain. These tests measure skills that are not learned, but spring from the inherent physical foundation of intelligent functioning. The tests in this chapter measure long-term and short-term memory, the ability to recognize similarities and differences, synaptic speed and accuracy, and the ability to focus through distraction.

The idea of an overall IQ is very controversial and elusive. The IQ is made up of varying levels of specific skills that are as individual as fingerprints; and in the final analysis, the intellect is only as valuable as the use to which it is put. When we set out to judge the intelligence of others we look for such qualities as verbal abilities, problem-solving skills, social competence, and interest in learning. When someone is accomplished in these areas we think of him as very intelligent. While all of these qualities *do* point to someone who is likely to have a high IQ, psychologists believe the key to the truly intelligent person is his level of motivation. The type of motivation to which they refer cannot be measured by any particular test but can only be observed in an individual's behavior, in his attitudes toward life, and in his approach to problems. In fact, someone who reads a book like *The Brain Game* is demonstrating intellectual curiosity and that all-important motivation which is the mark of real intelligence.

By now you are probably ready to get started. You will need only a pencil and a timer or clock. We recommend that you begin with Test 1 to get a straightforward look at your overall intelligence. Then take the chapters in any order that interests you. If you do not already know where your true talents lie, by the time you finish taking the tests in this book you'll have a fairly accurate profile of your intellectual strengths.

1. IQ Test

Through the eight decades since French psychologist Alfred Binet accepted the challenge to develop a measure of intelligence, over 200 intelligence tests have been created. Each reflects its creator's view of the best way to measure intellectual functioning. The diversity of intelligence tests demonstrates the concern — and confusion — that is focused on defining the concept of intelligence. As one test developer wrote, ''The nature of intelligence has been a favorite subject for contemplation and disputation for centuries — perhaps from the dawn of man as *Homo sapiens*. The topic is being studied and debated today by educators, sociologists, geneticists, neurophysiologists, and biochemists, and by psychologists specializing in various branches of the discipline.''

Almost everyone agrees that intelligence is a good thing to have. We assume that higher intelligence is associated with many of the good things in life, such as higher income, higher status, and social attractiveness. And we usually feel that we can tell who among our acquaintances is and is not intelligent. But what is being measured when we take an intelligence test?

The question reflects a long-waged battle within psychology and education. For many years, intelligence was seen by psychologists primarily as a broad and general skill. Then others began to test it as a series of 120 narrow, specific functions. The controversy is complicated by views of the basis of intelligence as totally inherited versus totally environmental. The best guess is that intelligence is a composite of several major abilities, partly inherited and partly determined by the environment. Your intelligence quotient is a way of summarizing these and other factors and representing intelligence in a simple numerical form.

The IQ test that follows was developed by Mensa, a national organization composed of people with superior levels of tested intelligence. The test will measure your verbal and spatial abilities, as well as your logical and problem-solving skills, and will serve as your introduction to some of the tests of specific abilities in *The Brain Game*.

INSTRUCTIONS

In the IQ Test you will be presented with 39 questions requiring various responses. Before you begin the test, tear out one of the Answer Sheets that follow and use it to record your responses. Some additional Answer Sheets are provided here so your friends may take the test as well.

Give yourself 30 minutes to complete the 39 items. When your time is up, stop your work and turn the page to find your score.

1. What number follows logically in this series?

    2, 3, 5, 9, 17, _____

2. In the group of words below, which two words are most nearly opposite in meaning?

   Example: *heavy*, large, flat, *light*, bright

   punish, vex, pinch, ignore, pacify, determine

3. Figure out the rule that is used to determine the prices below and find the price of the last item.

watch	$46
bracelet	$4
earrings	$10
chain	$6
ring	$?

4. Study the four drawings in the top row. Which of the four drawings in the bottom row should appear next in the series?

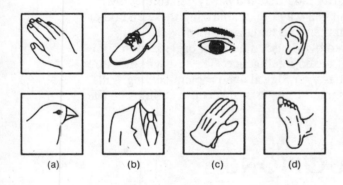

(a)   (b)   (c)   (d)

5. The arrows represent a simple code. What common English word do they spell?

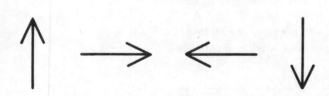

6. In the square below, a rule applies both from top to bottom and from left to right. Find the rule and figure out the missing number. Note: the example and the square below follow different rules.

Example:	2	7	9
	5	4	9
	7	11	18

6	2	4
2	?	0
4	0	4

7. Which drawing in the bottom row logically comes next in the series that is shown in the top row?

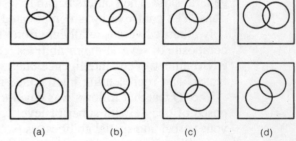

(a)   (b)   (c)   (d)

8. Complete this analogy by writing one word on the lines, ending with the printed letter.

   Lend is to *borrow* as *harmony*

   is to __ __ __ __ __ __d.

9. Which two words in parentheses have the same relation as the two words in the first phrase?

   Island is to *water* as

   (without, hypotenuse, center, diagonal, perimeter)

10. If Doris turns either left or right at the stop sign, she will run out of gas before reaching a service station. She has already gone too far past the last service station to turn around and return to it. She does not see a service station ahead of her. Therefore:
    (a) Doris may run out of gas.
    (b) Doris will run out of gas.
    (c) Doris should not have taken this route.

10

ANSWER SHEET

1. I Q Test

1. _____

2. _____ and _____

3. $_____

4. a 0
   b 0
   c 0
   d 0

5. _____

6. _____

7. a 0
   b 0
   c 0
   d 0

8. _ _ _ _ _ _ d

9. _____ is to _____

10. a 0
    b 0
    c 0

11. _____

12. a 0
    b 0
    c 0

13. a 0
    b 0
    c 0
    d 0

14. _____ and _____

15. a 0
    b 0
    c 0
    d 0

16. a 0
    b 0
    c 0
    d 0

17. a 0
    b 0
    c 0
    d 0

18. a 0
    b 0
    c 0
    d 0

19. a 0
    b 0
    c 0
    d 0

20. _____ and _____

21. $_____

22. a 0
    b 0
    c 0
    d 0

23. _____

24. a 0
    b 0
    c 0
    d 0

25. a 0
    b 0
    c 0
    d 0

26. a 0
    b 0
    c 0
    d 0
    e 0

27. a 0
    b 0
    c 0
    d 0

28. a 0
    b 0
    c 0
    d 0

29. _____ and _____

30. a 0
    b 0
    c 0
    d 0
    e 0

31. a 0
    b 0
    c 0
    d 0

32. a 0
    b 0
    c 0
    d 0

33. _____ and _____

34. _____

35. _____ is to _____

36. _ _ _ k

37. a 0
    b 0
    c 0
    d 0

38. a 0
    b 0
    c 0
    d 0

39. _____ is to _____

(Tear Out)

ANSWER SHEET

1. I Q Test

1. _____

2. _____ and _____

3. $_____

4. a 0
   b 0
   c 0
   d 0

5. _____

6. _____

7. a 0
   b 0
   c 0
   d 0

8. _ _ _ _ _ d

9. _____ is to _____

10. a 0
    b 0
    c 0

11. _____

12. a 0
    b 0
    c 0

13. a 0
    b 0
    c 0
    d 0

14. _____ and _____

15. a 0
    b 0
    c 0
    d 0

16. a 0
    b 0
    c 0
    d 0

17. a 0
    b 0
    c 0
    d 0

18. a 0
    b 0
    c 0
    d 0

19. a 0
    b 0
    c 0
    d 0

20. _____ and _____

21. $_____

22. a 0
    b 0
    c 0
    d 0

23. _____

24. a 0
    b 0
    c 0
    d 0

25. a 0
    b 0
    c 0
    d 0

26. a 0
    b 0
    c 0
    d 0
    e 0

27. a 0
    b 0
    c 0
    d 0

28. a 0
    b 0
    c 0
    d 0

29. _____ and _____

30. a 0
    b 0
    c 0
    d 0
    e 0

31. a 0
    b 0
    c 0
    d 0

32. a 0
    b 0
    c 0
    d 0

33. _____ and _____

34. _____

35. _____ is to _____

36. _ _ _ k

37. a 0
    b 0
    c 0
    d 0

38. a 0
    b 0
    c 0
    d 0

39. _____ is to _____

(Tear Out)

ANSWER SHEET

1. I Q Test

1. _____

2. _____ and _____

3. $_____

4. a 0
   b 0
   c 0
   d 0

5. _____

6. _____

7. a 0
   b 0
   c 0
   d 0

8. _ _ _ _ _ _ d

9. _____ is to _____

10. a 0
    b 0
    c 0

11. _____

12. a 0
    b 0
    c 0

13. a 0
    b 0
    c 0
    d 0

14. _____ and _____

15. a 0
    b 0
    c 0
    d 0

16. a 0
    b 0
    c 0
    d 0

17. a 0
    b 0
    c 0
    d 0

18. a 0
    b 0
    c 0
    d 0

19. a 0
    b 0
    c 0
    d 0

20. _____ and _____

21. $_____

22. a 0
    b 0
    c 0
    d 0

23. _____

24. a 0
    b 0
    c 0
    d 0

25. a 0
    b 0
    c 0
    d 0

26. a 0
    b 0
    c 0
    d 0
    e 0

27. a 0
    b 0
    c 0
    d 0

28. a 0
    b 0
    c 0
    d 0

29. _____ and _____

30. a 0
    b 0
    c 0
    d 0
    e 0

31. a 0
    b 0
    c 0
    d 0

32. a 0
    b 0
    c 0
    d 0

33. _____ and _____

34. _____

35. _____ is to _____

36. _ _ _ k

37. a 0
    b 0
    c 0
    d 0

38. a 0
    b 0
    c 0
    d 0

39. _____ is to _____

(Tear Out)

ANSWER SHEET

1. I Q Test

1. _____

2. _____ and _____

3. $_____

4. a 0
   b 0
   c 0
   d 0

5. _____

6. _____

7. a 0
   b 0
   c 0
   d 0

8. _ _ _ _ _ _ d

9. _____ is to _____

10. a 0
    b 0
    c 0

11. _____

12. a 0
    b 0
    c 0

13. a 0
    b 0
    c 0
    d 0

14. _____ and _____

15. a 0
    b 0
    c 0
    d 0

16. a 0
    b 0
    c 0
    d 0

17. a 0
    b 0
    c 0
    d 0

18. a 0
    b 0
    c 0
    d 0

19. a 0
    b 0
    c 0
    d 0

20. _____ and _____

21. $_____

22. a 0
    b 0
    c 0
    d 0

23. _____

24. a 0
    b 0
    c 0
    d 0

25. a 0
    b 0
    c 0
    d 0

26. a 0
    b 0
    c 0
    d 0
    e 0

27. a 0
    b 0
    c 0
    d 0

28. a 0
    b 0
    c 0
    d 0

29. _____ and _____

30. a 0
    b 0
    c 0
    d 0
    e 0

31. a 0
    b 0
    c 0
    d 0

32. a 0
    b 0
    c 0
    d 0

33. _____ and _____

34. _____

35. _____ is to _____

36. _ _ _ k

37. a 0
    b 0
    c 0
    d 0

38. a 0
    b 0
    c 0
    d 0

39. _____ is to _____

(Tear Out)

11. Find the number that logically completes this series:

1, 2, 6, 12, 36, _____

12. Which building in the bottom row logically comes next in the series that is shown in the top row?

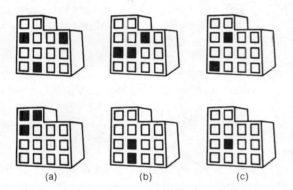

(a)   (b)   (c)

13. M is above N and O. N is above O and below P. Therefore:

    (a)   M is not above O and P.
    (b)   O is above N.
    (c)   P is above O.
    (d)   O is above P.

14. In the group of words below, which two words are most similar in meaning?

(Example: *mat,* linoleum, floor, *rug)*

beam, lump, wood, ray, chuckle, silver

15. Which figure in the lower row should appear next in the series of figures in the upper row?

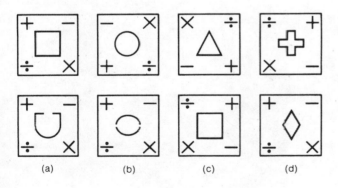

(a)   (b)   (c)   (d)

16. If $a \times b = 24$, $b \times c = 24$, $b \times d = 48$, and $c \times d = 32$, what then does $a \times b \times c \times d$ equal?

(a) 480   (b) 744   (c) 768   (d) 824

17. Complete the top series with one of the lettered figures from below.

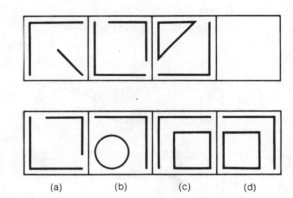

(a)   (b)   (c)   (d)

18. ''Don't throw good money after bad'' means:

    (a)   Take your loss and walk away from it.
    (b)   Don't gamble; think of the future.
    (c)   Don't invest in a losing proposition.
    (d)   Don't borrow to gamble.

19. Sam, Fred, Steve, and Joe are weight lifters. Joe can outlift Steve, and Fred can outlift Joe. Steve can outlift Sam. Therefore:

    (a)   Both Sam and Fred can outlift Joe.
    (b)   Joe can outlift Sam but can't outlift Steve.
    (c)   Joe can outlift Sam by more than he can outlift Steve.
    (d) None of the above is true.

20. Select the two figures in the following series that represent mirror images of each other.

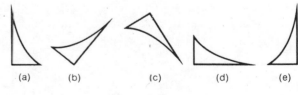

(a)   (b)   (c)   (d)   (e)

21. Determine what process was followed in arriving at the prices below and find the price of the last item.

skirt	$50
tie	$30
raincoat	$80
sweater	$70
blouse	$?

22. Which plate in the bottom row belongs next in the series in the top row?

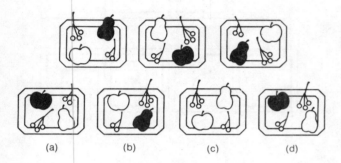

(a)   (b)   (c)   (d)

23. What number logically comes next in this series?

    7, 12, 27, 72, _____

24. The old saying "The good is the enemy of the best" most nearly means:

    (a) If you are good, you will best your enemy.
    (b) Be good to your best enemy.
    (c) Don't accept less than your best.
    (d) The good struggle against the best.

25.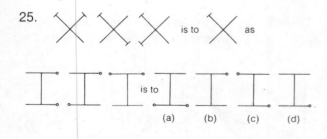

26. Alex, Allan, Carol, Celia, and Sharon took intelligence tests. Celia scored higher than Carol, but Allan scored higher than Celia. Carol outscored Alex, but Allan outscored Carol. Sharon scored lower than Allan. Therefore:

    (a) Celia scored higher than Alex but lower than Carol.
    (b) Both Alex and Allan outscored Celia.
    (c) Sharon scored higher than Carol.
    (d) Celia outscored Alex by more than she outscored Carol.
    (e) None of the above is definitely true.

27. What number follows logically in this series?

    9, 12, 21, 48, _____

    (a) 69 (b) 70 (c) 129 (d) 144

28. Which one of the lettered diagrams in the bottom row can be turned over or rotated to become the same as the diagram below?

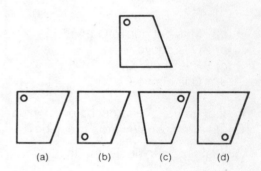

(a)   (b)   (c)   (d)

29. In the group of words below, choose the two words that are most nearly alike in meaning.

    tale, novel, volume, story, book

16

30. If Barbara's daughter is my daughter's mother, what am I to Barbara?

    (a) her grandmother
    (b) her mother
    (c) her daughter
    (d) her granddaughter
    (e) I am Barbara.

31. In a row of four houses, the Whites live next to the Carsons, but not next to the Reeds. If the Reeds do not live next to the Lanes, who are the Lanes' next-door neighbors?

    (a) the Whites
    (b) the Carsons
    (c) both the Whites and the Carsons
    (d) impossible to tell

32. *Wall* is to *window* as *face* is to

    (a) *skin*
    (b) *hair*
    (c) *eye*
    (d) *teeth*

33. Select the two figures in the following series that represent mirror images of each other.

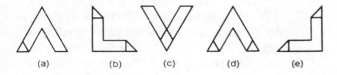

    (a)   (b)   (c)   (d)   (e)

34. What is the next number in this series?

    21, 20, 18, 15, 11, _____

35. Choose the two words in parentheses that have the same relation as the two words in the first phrase.

    Eyelid is to *eye* as

    (window, glass, view, curtain, lash)

36. Complete the following analogy by writing one word on the lines, ending with the printed letter.

    skull is to *brain* as *shell* is to __ __ __k.

37. Complete this diagram:

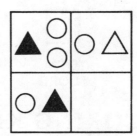

    (a)   (b)   (c)   (d)

38. "A stream cannot rise higher than its source" means:

    (a) You decline after achieving your highest level.
    (b) Streams of knowledge can't come from high sources.
    (c) Your stream of consciousness is highly resourceful.
    (d) Your stream of achievement is limited by your background.

39. Choose the two words in parentheses that have the same relation as the two words in the first phrase.

    Hat is to *head* as

    (spout, kettle, handle, copper, lid)

SCORING

Compare your answers on the Answer Sheet to the Scoring Key below. Give yourself 1 point for each correct answer and write the total in the box below.

TOTAL
SCORE

SCORING KEY

1. 33. Each increment is double the previous increment; or double each number and subtract 1 to get the next numbers.
2. vex, pacify. Although some of the other words have somewhat antithetical meanings, these two are considered most nearly opposite.
3. $36. The price is determined by the position in the alphabet of the initial letter of each item, multiplied by two — $2 for an item beginning with *a*, $4 for one starting with *b*, etc.
4. (b) right shoulder. Human things are alternated right and left. Although this item was missed by most Mensans, once it was explained, there was virtually no argument about the answer.
5. news. The arrows represent north, east, west, and south.
6. 20. In rows, the left number minus the middle number equals the right number. In columns, the top number minus the middle number equals the bottom number.
7. (a). The figure rotates counterclockwise by increments increasing one-eighth turn in each successive drawing. The second drawing has rotated one-eighth turn counterclockwise; the third has rotated an additional quarter turn; the fourth has rotated an additional three-eighths turn. The correct answer, (a), shows the figure rotated an additional four-eighths (one-half) turn.
8. discord
9. center, perimeter
10. (a). Not to see a gas station ahead doesn't mean there isn't one — it could be around a curve. So Doris may, or may not, run out of gas.
11. 72. Each succeeding number is alternately multiplied by 2 or 3.
12. (a). The black window on the far left side goes down one square each time before it starts again at the top; the black window in the middle goes up one square each time; the black window on the third floor moves left one square at a time.
13. (c)
14. beam, ray
15. (d). The center figure is always solid; the symbols in the corners are moving counterclockwise.
16. (c)
17. (d). The right angle is moving counterclockwise. The changing figure increases the number of its line segments by 1 in each succeeding square.
18. (a)
19. (c)
20. (a), (e)
21. $60. The price is determined by the number of letters in the word, multiplied by 10.
22. (a). The apple and pear alternate in color and are moving counterclockwise. The two bunches of cherries are moving clockwise.
23. 207. Each succeeding interval is multiplied by 3 and added to the subsequent number.
24. (c)
25. (b). The second dot moves clockwise and is "hidden" in the fourth drawing.
26. (d)
27. (c). Each increment is multiplied by 3 and added to the subsequent number.
28. (b)
29. tale, story
30. (c)
31. (a)
32. (c). This item was the "easiest" on the test. Still, one Mensan missed it.
33. (b), (e)
34. 6. Each number is reduced by a number that is increased by 1 with each succeeding term.
35. curtain, window
36. yolk
37. (a). Each square is exactly like its diagonal counterpart, except the color of the triangle changes from black to white or white to black.
38. (d)
39. lid, kettle

INTERPRETATION

Keep in mind as you interpret your performance on the IQ Test that your score is only an estimate of how intelligent you may be. Not everyone does his or her best at all times, and even the most accurately administered two-hour IQ test has what is called a probable error amount in any given score. That is why most professionals choose to interpret a score as equaling a range of IQ's and not as one single number. With that in mind, convert your test score to an IQ range as follows:

- With a score of 12 to 15, your IQ is probably in the 111-to-117 range, well into the top half of all adults.
- A score of 16 to 19 suggests an IQ in the range of 118 to 124, a strong performance.
- A score of 20 to 23 indicates an IQ of 125 to 131, quite good work.
- A score of 24 to 28 corresponds to an IQ of 132 to 139, a very high ability level in the top 5 percent of all adults.
- A score of 29 to 33 translates into an IQ range of 140 to 147, a level consistent with that scored by members of the Mensa organization and in the top 2 percent of adults.
- A score of 34 or above suggests an IQ of 148 or higher, an extremely strong showing on this test and in the top fraction of 1 percent of all adults.

As we mentioned in our introduction to this test, the IQ merely serves to summarize how you performed on this test at this time in your life. Another day — another test — could produce somewhat different results. But a strong performance here does suggest a high level of intellectual functioning across several ability areas. Other tests in *The Brain Game* assess those abilities in depth.

To gain a better idea of the tests that follow, look back over the IQ Test problems. Mentally group, for example, numbers 1, 6, 7, and 16. These problems measure your linear aptitude, the ability to go from one step to the next, to the next, in order to complete a sequence and solve the problem. Numbers 10 and 30 test your formal-logic skills — that is, how well you can solve a problem using inductive or deductive reasoning. All of these abilities are measured in Chapter One.

Problems 20, 28, and 33, on the other hand, involve spatial abilities, the skills involved in forming and rotating a mental representation of an object. This is similar to the ability required to create a mental image of a finished house from a set of two-dimensional plans. These and other conceptual skills are measured in Chapter Two.

Other problems, such as numbers 4, 8, 13, and 24, call for a synthesis of diverse mental skills. Your ability to combine your mental skills is measured in Chapter Three.

Your abilities in test taking — that is, working quickly under timed conditions, remembering formulas for similar types of questions, and recognizing similarities and differences — affect your final score on this and other tests. These abilities are measured in Chapter Four.

The 26 tests that follow will cause you to feel rushed and stimulated, frustrated and encouraged, and, it is hoped, will help you to learn a little more about your aptitudes and abilities. By pinpointing those specific areas in which you excel, you can discover your real intellectual strengths and learn how to use them to your advantage.

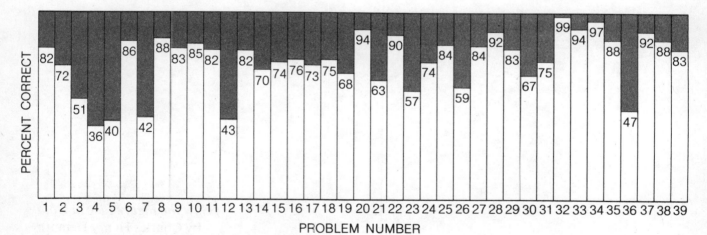

This chart shows the percentage of Mensa test takers that achieved the correct answer on each of the 39 questions in Test 1. Problem 32 was clearly the "easiest" question, while number 4 was missed by almost two thirds of those tested.

I Saw the Figure Five in Gold
by Charles Henry Demuth
The Metropolitan Museum of Art
New York

CHAPTER ONE

THE LEFT
HEMISPHERE

used in the treatment of epilepsy, psychologists have made a major breakthrough in mapping and understanding the intellectual functions of the human mind. The operation involves severing the tissue, called the corpus callosum, between the two hemispheres of the brain, leaving them, literally, unconnected. Its implementation since the 1960's has given psychologists, such as the Nobel Prize winner Roger Sperry, their first group of "split-brain" subjects. In experiments with these subjects, psychologists were able to study the differences between the right and left hemispheres of the brain and the way these hemispheres affect the human intellect.

What they found were some very specific and surprising differences between the two sides of the brain. You might say that the two hemispheres seem to have different ways of knowing the same information: the right is oriented toward visual, intuitive, holistic understanding, while the left is verbal and analytical, and it handles information in a sequential, logical manner. Both language and mathematics are left-brain skills, and this hemisphere excels in classifying objects in standard, linguistically defined categories. In fact, it is totally absorbed in organizing the parts and may never have a sense of the whole. That's where the right hemisphere comes in.

One interesting experiment that has been used to pinpoint the activity of the different hemispheres came out of observation of eye movement. When an individual is asked a question such as "How do you spell Massachusetts?" his eyes shift to the side as he searches for the answer. Psychologists Marcel Kinsbourne of Duke University and Katherine Kocel, David Galin, and Robert Ornstein of the Langly Porter Institute have found that the direction in which a person shifts his or her eyes is affected by the type of question asked. If the problem is linear-verbal (for instance, divide 144 by 6 and multiply the answer by 7), more eye movements are made to the right than if the question involves spatial analysis (such as, which way does Lincoln face on a penny?). The gaze to the right indicates a left-hemisphere search.

Schools tend to spend most of their time training students in what seem to be left-brain skills. The tests in this section will measure the extent of your abilities in this area. Some of the tests are among the most difficult in *The Brain Game* because they require certain mathematical knowledge and highly developed verbal and logical skills. Such left-hemisphere abilities represent the classic profile of what our culture regards as true intelligence. If you do score high on the next six tests, then you probably have a fairly high IQ and are oriented toward occupations that utilize your intellectual skills. Yet regardless of your scores on these tests, keep in mind that your abilities and skills must be measured in the other chapters of the book in order to analyze your overall aptitudes and intelligence.

2. Computer Science Aptitude Test

by J. Konvalina, L. Stephens, and S. Wileman

Most futurists believe that within the next 10 years more than half of the homes in America will be equipped with a household computer. We know for sure that businesses centered on this "computer revolution" are enjoying tremendous economic success and that the demand for computer professionals is very intense.

Computer-related jobs encompass such areas as computer programming and software development, computer hardware design, and microwave technology. Schools offering computer science courses have high enrollments in current classes and report increased demand for course variety. Schools and corporations that offer training programs for computer personnel have discovered that most of those who are able to complete the course successfully have fairly specific qualities to begin with.

Drs. John Konvalina, Larry Stephens, and Stanley Wileman, of the computer science program at the University of Nebraska at Omaha, wrote in 1981: "One of the major problems confronting educators in computer science and data processing is determining factors that influence success in beginning courses. The rapid increase in the need for personnel in these areas is attracting many individuals needing education, and the number who will not succeed with this education will increase."

As part of their involvement in computer science education, Drs. Konvalina, Stephens, and Wileman developed the Computer Science Aptitude Test. They proposed that the test be used to decide which applicants have a high likelihood of success in computer courses. In this way, high-level technical resources can be used more cost-effectively.

INSTRUCTIONS

To take the Computer Science Aptitude Test, turn the page and remove the Answer Sheet that you will use to record your responses. There is space on the Answer Sheet you can use to calculate your answers.

There are 25 questions on the test and you will have 40 minutes in which to complete it. When your time is up, stop your work and turn the page to calculate your score.

For questions 1 through 4, look for a pattern and fill in the missing term in the sequence:

1. A, C, F, H, K, M, _____
   (a) N   (b) O   (c) P   (d) Q   (e) R

2. ABC, ABD, ABE, ACD, ACE, _____
   (a) ADE   (b) ACB   (c) AED   (d) ADC   (e) AEC

3. $\frac{1}{4}$, $\frac{3}{6}$, $\frac{2}{5}$, $\frac{4}{7}$, $\frac{3}{6}$, _____
   (a) $\frac{1}{2}$ (b) $\frac{3}{8}$ (c) $\frac{4}{5}$ (d) $\frac{5}{8}$ (e) $\frac{2}{5}$

4. 1, 1, 2, 3, 5, 8, _____
   (a) 13   (b) 8   (c) 11   (d) 9   (e) 40

5. How many numbers are there in the sequence below if all the missing terms (indicated by ...) are included?

   0, 3, 6, 9, 12, 15, ..., 240

   (a) 240   (b) 241   (c) 80   (d) 81   (e) none of these

6. A teacher said to a student, "If you receive an A on the final exam, then you will pass the course." Suppose the student did not pass the course. What conclusion is valid?

   (a)   The student received an A on the final exam.
   (b)   The student did not receive an A on the final exam.
   (c)   The student flunked the final exam.
   (d)   If the student passed the course, then he or she received an A on the final.
   (e)   None of these is valid.

7. John said to Jane, "If it rains, then I won't play tennis." Suppose it did not rain; then what conclusion is valid?

   (a)   John played tennis.
   (b)   John did not play tennis.
   (c)   If John does not play tennis, then it rains.
   (d)   It did not rain and John played tennis.
   (e)   None of these is valid.

8. Suppose all computers are logical devices, and some computers are bistable. What conclusion is valid?

   (a)   All logical devices are bistable.
   (b)   All computers are bistable.
   (c)   Some computers are not logical devices.
   (d)   Some logical devices are computers.
   (e)   None of these is valid.

9. Think of a number. Add 3 to the number. Multiply your answer by 2. Subtract 4 from your answer. Divide by 2. Subtract the number with which you started. Your answer is

   (a) 0   (b) 1   (c) 2   (d) negative   (e) none of these

10. Which one of the words does not belong to the group?

   (a) REDDER   (b) BETTER   (c) RADAR

   (d) PEEP   (e) POP

ANSWER SHEET

2. Computer Science Aptitude Test

	a	b	c	d	e			a	b	c	d	e
1.	0	0	0	0	0		14.	0	0	0	0	0
2.	0	0	0	0	0		15.	0	0	0	0	0
3.	0	0	0	0	0		16.	0	0	0	0	0
4.	0	0	0	0	0		17.	0	0	0	0	0
5.	0	0	0	0	0		18.	0	0	0	0	0
6.	0	0	0	0	0		19.	0	0	0	0	0
7.	0	0	0	0	0		20.	0	0	0	0	0
8.	0	0	0	0	0		21.	0	0	0	0	0
9.	0	0	0	0	0		22.	0	0	0	0	0
10.	0	0	0	0	0		23.	0	0	0	0	0
11.	0	0	0	0	0		24.	0	0	0	0	0
12.	0	0	0	0	0		25.	0	0	0	0	0
13.	0	0	0	0	0							

NOTES

(Tear Out)

ANSWER SHEET

2. Computer Science Aptitude Test

	a	b	c	d	e			a	b	c	d	e
1.	O	O	O	O	O	14.	O	O	O	O	O
2.	O	O	O	O	O	15.	O	O	O	O	O
3.	O	O	O	O	O	16.	O	O	O	O	O
4.	O	O	O	O	O	17.	O	O	O	O	O
5.	O	O	O	O	O	18.	O	O	O	O	O
6.	O	O	O	O	O	19.	O	O	O	O	O
7.	O	O	O	O	O	20.	O	O	O	O	O
8.	O	O	O	O	O	21.	O	O	O	O	O
9.	O	O	O	O	O	22.	O	O	O	O	O
10.	O	O	O	O	O	23.	O	O	O	O	O
11.	O	O	O	O	O	24.	O	O	O	O	O
12.	O	O	O	O	O	25.	O	O	O	O	O
13.	O	O	O	O	O						

NOTES

(Tear Out)

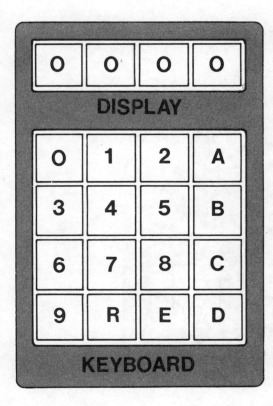

Consider the calculator shown here with a four-digit display, digits 0 through 9, and operations A, B, C, D, E, and R. The meaning of the operations of the calculator are as follows:

R = Reset the display so that all digits are 0.

E = Enter the number pressed after the letter E into the display.

A = Add the number pressed after the letter A to the number in the display and display the result (sum).

B = Subtract the number in the display from the number pressed after the letter B and display the result (difference).

C = Multiply the number pressed after the letter C by the number in the display and display the result (product).

D = Divide the number pressed after the letter D into the number in the display and display the result (whole-number quotient).

Note: Except for the letter R, a number is pressed after a letter.

An example of a calculator program is the following (instructions are performed from left to right in order): RE20B50D6. This program first resets the display to 0, then enters the number 20 into the display, subtracts 20 from 50 (the display now reads 30), and finally divides the result in the display by 6. The display reads 5 after the last operation.

Now answer the following questions based on the calculator above:

11. A student scored 85, 66, and 92 on three exams. Which calculator program will display the average of the three exams after the last operation?

(a) RE85A66B92D3
(b) RE85A66D3A92
(c) RE92A66A85D3
(d) RE92A66A85C3
(e) none of these

12. Mrs. Gross bought four single grocery items at the following prices: 69 cents, 45 cents, 12 cents, 37 cents. Also, she bought 5 pounds of bananas at 39 cents a pound. She paid for the groceries with a $10 bill (1,000 cents). Which calculator program will display her correct change (in cents)?

(a) RE69A45A12A39B1000
(b) RE39C5A69A45A12B1000
(c) RE69A45A12A37A39C5B1000
(d) RE5C39A69A45A12A37B1000
(e) none of these

13. Find the number displayed after the last operation of the following calculator program:

RE6A0B8C2C4D16B1

(a) 2 (b) 0 (c) 1 (d) a negative number
(e) none of these

14. Which statement best describes the following calculator program?

RE13D3C3B13

(a) divides two numbers, 13 and 3, and displays the quotient
(b) divides, multiplies the result, and finally displays 13 again
(c) computes and finally displays a negative number
(d) computes and displays 3 times 13 minus 13
(e) computes and displays the remainder when 13 is divided by 3

15. What last operation must be added to the following program so that the display will read 1 after the last operation?

RE12A3C2B56D2 _____

(a) D14 (b) A1 (c) B13 (d) B12 (e) none of these

27

Assume we have four light bulbs arranged in a circle labeled 1, 2, 3, and 4 as shown in the figure.

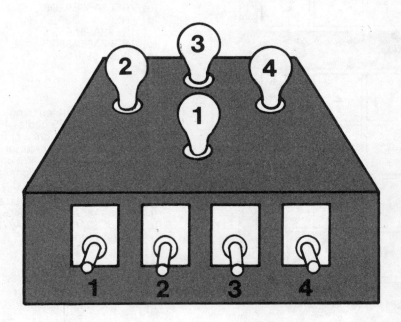

Assume further that we have four switches connected so that each switch controls the light bulb with the corresponding number. Consider the following set of instructions, but do not perform the actions indicated yet.

1. *Turn on the light bulb that is directly across from the single light bulb that is on.*
2. *If any odd-numbered light bulb is on, go to step 4.*
3. *Turn off the lowest-numbered light bulb, and go to step 5.*
4. *Turn off the highest-numbered light bulb.*
5. *Turn on the bulb next to the highest-numbered bulb that is on, in a clockwise direction.*
6. *Turn off any even-numbered bulbs which might be on, and stop.*

Now answer the following questions:

16. Assume only light bulb 1 is on. Carry out the instructions, starting with step 1. When you stop in step 6,

    (a) light bulbs 3 and 4 are on
    (b) no light bulbs are on
    (c) only light bulb 1 is on
    (d) only light bulb 2 is on
    (e) none of the above

17. Carry out the instructions again. This time assume only light bulb 2 is on at the beginning. When you stop in step 6,

    (a) only light bulb 1 is on
    (b) light bulbs 2 and 3 are on
    (c) at least three light bulbs are on
    (d) only two light bulbs are on
    (e) none of the above

18. Again carry out the instructions, this time assuming only light bulb 3 is on initially. When you stop in step 6,

   (a) only bulb 2 is on
   (b) only bulb 3 is on
   (c) only bulb 4 is on
   (d) all bulbs are on
   (e) none of the above

19. Finally, carry out the instructions assuming only bulb 4 is initially on. When you stop in step 6,

   (a) light bulbs 2 and 4 are on
   (b) light bulbs 1 and 3 are on
   (c) at least one even-numbered bulb is on
   (d) at least one odd-numbered bulb is on
   (e) none of the above

20. Based on your experience in carrying out the instructions,

   (a) the instructions can be applied regardless of the number of light bulbs initially turned on
   (b) regardless of which light bulb is initially on, when we stop in step 6 all light bulbs will be off
   (c) regardless of which light bulb is initially on, when we stop in step 6 only light bulb 1 will be on
   (d) when an even-numbered bulb is initially turned on, then when we stop in step 6 only light bulb 3 will be on
   (e) none of the above

PART IV
(Word Problems)

21. Six times a number is 3 more than twice the number. What is the number?

   (a) $^4/_3$ (b) $-\frac{3}{4}$ (c) $\frac{3}{4}$ (d) $-4\frac{1}{2}$
   (e) none of these

22. A bank contains nickels and dimes. The total value of the coins is $2.10 and there are three more dimes than nickels. How many nickels are there?

   (a) 13 (b) 12 (c) 15 (d) 36 (e) none of these

23. A law requires that the amount of chicken used in hot dogs cannot exceed 25 percent of the total weight of the hot dog. How many ounces could a hot dog weigh if it contained 1.5 ounces of chicken?

   (a) 3 (b) 5 (c) 5.5 (d) 6 (e) none of these

24. A farmer mixes seed worth 15 cents per pound with seed worth 20 cents per pound to produce a mixture of 50 pounds of seed worth 18 cents per pound. How many pounds of seed worth 20 cents per pound did he use in the mixture?

   (a) 20 (b) 25 (c) 30 (d) 40 (e) none of these

25. Volumes 12 through 29 of an encyclopedia have misprints on pages 21 through 53 of each volume. How many pages in the encyclopedia have misprints?

   (a) 18 (b) 32 (c) 544 (d) 594 (e) none of these

SCORING

To score this test, compare your responses on the Answer Sheet to those that appear on the Scoring Key below. Give yourself 1 point for each correct answer and write the total in the box below.

TOTAL
SCORE

SCORING KEY

1.	c	14.	c
2.	a	15.	e
3.	d	16.	c
4.	a	17.	a
5.	d	18.	e
6.	b	19.	d
7.	e	20.	c
8.	d	21.	c
9.	b	22.	b
10.	b	23.	d
11.	c	24.	c
12.	d	25.	d
13.	b		

INTERPRETATION

The Computer Science Aptitude Test is intended for just that purpose — the measurement of aptitude in computer science and the probability of success in related courses. As it is used in some universities, people who score below average are permitted to enroll only in nontechnical "computer appreciation" courses involving little, if any, computer-language and programming training. If they demonstrate success in learning the material, they are then allowed to register for increasingly advanced courses.

If you scored between 0 and 20 you demonstrated a low-to-average level of the basic computer-related skills that research has shown to predict success in computer courses. If you scored low and do happen to be intrigued by computers or have thought about pursuing the field as a career, you should plan carefully. Increase your level of understanding about the computer-related jobs and training programs that are available. Investigate computer applications that more closely relate to skills that you scored high on in *The Brain Game*.

If you've scored low to average here but very high on tests measuring spatial or artistic skills, for example, you may be in a situation similar to the person who cannot assemble or repair cameras but who takes award-winning photographs. An ability to use computers is not the same as the abilities to understand their operation and program them.

An above-average to very high score on this test, 21 to 25, is associated with a high potential for success in technical computer courses. These courses often include learning one or more of the computer languages, such as BASIC or FORTRAN, and applying the language in writing computer programs.

3. Analysis-of-Explanations Test

The ability to analyze and understand logical principles is not a simple matter of memorizing and applying straightforward formulas. Each of the questions in the Analysis-of-Explanations Test involves certain principles of reasoning that need to be understood in terms of how each principle works in the given situation. Frequently, the results of the situations presented in the test are unexpected; they will test your ability to select a reason that can explain the unexpected result. Since the apparent contradiction will often be based on a minor detail in the situation, answering the questions correctly will require you to put together various bits of information logically.

As with many tests that measure logical skills, the Analysis-of-Explanations Test requires a working familiarity with the principles involved. To make the most of the skills centered in your left hemisphere, study the Instructions *and* the sample questions in depth. To do well on the test, you will need to fully understand the principles of logic that are presented.

INSTRUCTIONS

This test consists of four sets of questions. In each set, a fact-situation and a result are presented. Ten numbered statements follow the result. You are to evaluate each of the statements in relation to the fact-situation and result. Evaluate the statements using the sequence of decisions in the next column. Do your evaluation in the order (a), (b), (c), (d), (e). *The first of these that you cannot eliminate is the answer. Study carefully the example on the facing page before you begin the test.*

When you are ready to start, turn the page and tear out the Answer Sheet that you will use to record your responses. Give yourself 25 minutes to complete the test. When your time is up, stop your work and turn the page to find your score.

(a) *First ask if the statement is* **inconsistent** *with, or contradicts, the fact-situation, the result, or both together. If so, choose* (a). *If not, proceed.*

(b) *Does the statement present a* **possible adequate explanation** *of the result? If so, choose* (b). *If not, proceed.*

(c) *Ask whether the* **statement must be true** *if the fact-situation and result are as stated. Thus if the statement is* **deducible** *from something in the fact-situation, the result, or both together, your answer should be* (c). *If it is not deducible, proceed.*

(d) *If the statement* **either supports or weakens** *a possible explanation of the result, if it is* **relevant** *to an explanation, you should choose* (d). *If not, proceed.*

(e) *If the statement is* **irrelevant** *to an explanation of the result, choose* (e).

© 1980 Arco Publishing, Inc. From The Graduate Record Examination Aptitude Test by the Arco Editorial Board.

EXAMPLE

THE PROBLEM

SITUATION: As far back as the Kung Bushmen could remember, the antelope had roamed the steppe land bordering the Kalahari Desert in South Africa. As the human population pressure forced the Kung deeper into the desert, they became more and more dependent upon hunting the antelope until they were hunting almost as many antelope as the antelope's greatest predator, the lion. Because the central government was alarmed that the antelope herds would disappear entirely, they established a park in the steppe country where antelope could not be hunted. The Kung were angry but could not oppose this new government policy. Enforcement was maintained by armed guards who patrolled the southern border daily in jeeps. This policy successfully prevented the Kung from hunting antelope.

RESULT: The antelope continued to diminish at an alarming rate.

STATEMENTS:

1. The government was more powerful than the Kung Bushmen.

2. The Kung are famous in the anthropological literature as the most adroit of all African peoples in tracking and hunting wild animals.

3. Park guards provided food and water for the antelope.

4. There was a severe drought which killed off 90 percent of all wildlife in the steppe.

5. The Kung realized that the ban on hunting antelope was reasonable and just.

THE ANSWERS

1. **(c).** This statement is not inconsistent with the information given and does not explain why the antelope herds continued to diminish. It is, however, deducible from the fact that the government was able to establish a park for antelope and prevent the Kung from hunting. The correct answer is (c).

2. **(e).** This statement is not inconsistent with the passage and does not explain why the antelope continued to diminish at an alarming rate. The passage clearly indicates that the Kung were no longer able to hunt. Thus their hunting prowess cannot possibly explain the result. There is no information in the passage which allows us to deduce that the Kung are the most adroit hunters of all African peoples. Since the result must be explained by something other than hunting the statement neither supports nor weakens the result. The correct answer therefore is (e); the statement is irrelevant to an explanation of the result.

3. **(d).** This information is not inconsistent with the information given. It neither explains why the antelope continued to diminish nor is it deducible. It is irrelevant to a possible explanation, namely that the antelope lacked sufficient food to survive. It weakens this possible explanation. Therefore the correct answer is (d).

4. **(b).** This statement is not inconsistent with information given and provides a possible adequate explanation for the continued decrease of the antelope population. The correct answer is (b).

5. **(a).** This statement is inconsistent with the fact that the Kung were angry at the hunting ban and that the ban had to be enforced with armed guards. The correct answer is (a).

SET 1

SITUATION: More than half the families of Steep Valley were farmers and those who weren't depended upon the auxiliary farm services for their livelihood. For as long as the farmers of Steep Valley could remember, their principal cash crop had been wheat. Even in years of a wheat glut, wheat paid — thanks to the government price support. In the past three years, however, wheat production per acre had dropped by 50 percent. The farmers faced a crisis and would be out of business if the output per acre dropped any lower. An agronomist from Washington was hired and reported that the soil had been depleted. He recommended that the farmers switch to soybeans, a crop which would have immediate high yields while simultaneously replenishing the soil. The price of soybeans was high and the farmers converted all land planted in wheat to soybeans.

RESULT: Within three years all 50 farmers in Steep Valley had closed their farms for good.

1. The price of soybeans rose significantly.

2. The soybean seed purchased by the farmers was contaminated with a fungus that made the soil permanently infertile.

3. The price supports for wheat were abolished.

4. The farmers did not follow the agronomist's advice.

5. The agronomist believed that the drop in wheat production was due to soil depletion.

6. All 600 families in Steep Valley had to apply for government relief.

7. Soybeans require five times as much water as wheat.

8. A federal dam project flooded Steep Valley as Boulder River was diverted to create an artificial lake.

9. The farmers in Steep Valley were not afraid to take drastic measures to keep their farms in business.

10. Throughout the state, Steep Valley wheat was known for its superior quality.

SET 2

SITUATION: The financial advisory board of Clover Canyon Women's College convened for an emergency session on August 14, 1965. Clover Canyon had always been known as a prestigious, small school with the major portion of its attendees from the surrounding area — Fernwood, South Carolina. The topic of the meeting was the school's decreased enrollment and subsequent lack of funds. Mr. Julip, the board's president, proposed a solution to the problem. He suggested admitting men during the 1966 fall term. He felt that this measure would increase enrollment by 50 percent. Mr. Julip pointed out that Ruby Falls, a women's college in Brooklyn, New York, had "gone coed" in 1964 and had thereby gained an additional $1.5 million in revenue. The board voted unanimously to turn Clover Canyon into a coed college, but decided to phase men in over a three-year period.

RESULT: In 1974, Clover Canyon was still a women's college.

11. Because Ruby Falls was a southern school and conservative in its outlook, the alumni disapproved of its new coeducational admissions policy.

12. In the five-year period from 1965 to 1970, seven Clover Canyon students won National Merit Scholarships.

13. The governing board of Clover Canyon was against a coeducational school.

14. South Carolina had an unusually cold winter in 1966.

15. Although Clover Canyon had always been small, it was felt that additional funds could be raised by increasing enrollment.

16. The student senate organized a strike in which a large percentage of the student body participated, which publicized the students' opposition to the new coeducational admissions policy.

17. In September of 1965, Clover Canyon received a grant of $500,000.

18. Most of Clover Canyon's students were from the Midwest and California.

19. Daisy Hill, a women's college in Texas, went coed in 1965.

20. The financial board felt that admitting men was a feasible way of obtaining additional necessary funds.

ANSWER SHEET

3. Analysis-of-Explanations Test

(a) First ask if the statement is *inconsistent* with, or contradicts, the fact-situation, the result, or both together. If so, choose (a). If not, proceed.

(b) Does the statement present a *possible adequate explanation* of the result? If so, choose (b). If not, proceed.

(c) Ask whether the *statement must be true* if the fact-situation and results are as stated. Thus if the statement is *deducible* from something in the fact-situation, the result, or both together, your answer should be (c). If it is not deducible, proceed.

(d) If the statement *either supports or weakens* a possible explanation of the result, that is, if it is *relevant* to an explanation, you should choose (d). If not, proceed.

(e) If the statement is *irrelevant* to an explanation of the result, choose (e).

	a b c d e		a b c d e		a b c d e
1.	0 0 0 0 0	14.	0 0 0 0 0	28.	0 0 0 0 0
2.	0 0 0 0 0	15.	0 0 0 0 0	29.	0 0 0 0 0
3.	0 0 0 0 0	16.	0 0 0 0 0	30.	0 0 0 0 0
4.	0 0 0 0 0	17.	0 0 0 0 0	31.	0 0 0 0 0
5.	0 0 0 0 0	18.	0 0 0 0 0	32.	0 0 0 0 0
6.	0 0 0 0 0	19.	0 0 0 0 0	33.	0 0 0 0 0
7.	0 0 0 0 0	20.	0 0 0 0 0	34.	0 0 0 0 0
8.	0 0 0 0 0	21.	0 0 0 0 0	35.	0 0 0 0 0
9.	0 0 0 0 0	22.	0 0 0 0 0	36.	0 0 0 0 0
10.	0 0 0 0 0	23.	0 0 0 0 0	37.	0 0 0 0 0
11.	0 0 0 0 0	24.	0 0 0 0 0	38.	0 0 0 0 0
12.	0 0 0 0 0	25.	0 0 0 0 0	39.	0 0 0 0 0
13.	0 0 0 0 0	26.	0 0 0 0 0	40.	0 0 0 0 0
		27.	0 0 0 0 0		

(Tear Out)

ANSWER SHEET

3. Analysis-of-Explanations Test

(a) First ask if the statement is _inconsistent_ with, or contradicts, the fact-situation, the result, or both together. If so, choose (a). If not, proceed.

(b) Does the statement present a _possible adequate explanation_ of the result? If so, choose (b). If not, proceed.

(c) Ask whether the _statement must be true_ if the fact-situation and results are as stated. Thus if the statement is _deducible_ from something in the fact-situation, the result, or both together, your answer should be (c). If it is not deducible, proceed.

(d) If the statement _either supports or weakens_ a possible explanation of the result, that is, if it is _relevant_ to an explanation, you should choose (d). If not, proceed.

(e) If the statement is _irrelevant_ to an explanation of the result, choose (e).

	a	b	c	d	e		a	b	c	d	e		a	b	c	d	e
1.	O	O	O	O	O	14.	O	O	O	O	O	28.	O	O	O	O	O
2.	O	O	O	O	O	15.	O	O	O	O	O	29.	O	O	O	O	O
3.	O	O	O	O	O	16.	O	O	O	O	O	30.	O	O	O	O	O
4.	O	O	O	O	O	17.	O	O	O	O	O	31.	O	O	O	O	O
5.	O	O	O	O	O	18.	O	O	O	O	O	32.	O	O	O	O	O
6.	O	O	O	O	O	19.	O	O	O	O	O	33.	O	O	O	O	O
7.	O	O	O	O	O	20.	O	O	O	O	O	34.	O	O	O	O	O
8.	O	O	O	O	O	21.	O	O	O	O	O	35.	O	O	O	O	O
9.	O	O	O	O	O	22.	O	O	O	O	O	36.	O	O	O	O	O
10.	O	O	O	O	O	23.	O	O	O	O	O	37.	O	O	O	O	O
11.	O	O	O	O	O	24.	O	O	O	O	O	38.	O	O	O	O	O
12.	O	O	O	O	O	25.	O	O	O	O	O	39.	O	O	O	O	O
13.	O	O	O	O	O	26.	O	O	O	O	O	40.	O	O	O	O	O
						27.	O	O	O	O	O						

(Tear Out)

SET 3

SITUATION: Ms. Moneybright, despite her successful career as a Wall Street broker for the firm of Dollars & Bills, was dissatisfied with her work. She had gotten her B.A. in American literature and had always wanted to be an editor or a writer. As a broker she made a great deal of money but never had time for serious reading, let alone writing. When *The Financial Wizard* offered Ms. Moneybright a full-time job as financial editor of their monthly magazine, she immediately wrote them a letter accepting their offer.

RESULT: That June, Ms. Moneybright celebrated her 15th anniversary as an employee of Dollars & Bills.

21. Ms. Moneybright wrote her college thesis on metaphor and allegory in *Moby Dick*.

22. Ms. Moneybright was offered a substantial raise to stay with Dollars & Bills.

23. *The Financial Wizard* went out of business because of bankruptcy.

24. Ms. Moneybright fell in love with the president of Dollars & Bills.

25. The staff of *The Financial Wizard* was sued for libel for a series of articles exposing unethical practices by brokerage firms.

26. Ms. Moneybright was functionally illiterate.

27. *The Financial Wizard* was sold to the firm of Dollars & Bills.

28. Ms. Moneybright was qualified to work as an editor.

29. Ms. Moneybright's only goal in working was to earn a great deal of money.

30. Ms. Moneybright did not know how to type.

SET 4

SITUATION: Because caviar is packaged in small containers, it is very easy to steal. Mr. Luxe, the owner of the Lush Goods gourmet store, discovered, while going over his store's inventory during the spring, that he had to replace 6 cases of Russian caviar, 4 of Finnish, and 10 of American. When he checked his books, he discovered that only 16 cases of caviar had been paid for. Mr. Luxe was extremely disappointed with his loss because caviar was his highest-priced item of merchandise. In order to prevent such losses in the future, Mr. Luxe moved the caviar into the cheese section of his store so that the customers would have to request and pay for the caviar at the same time. Mr. Luxe also required that customers check packages at the entrance.

RESULT: The following spring, during his inventory check, Mr. Luxe discovered that six cases of caviar were missing which had not been paid for.

31. Because of Mr. Luxe's precautions, the caviar theft rate was lowered.

32. In each case of caviar there were 15 individual jars.

33. Because Mr. Luxe's champagne was his highest-priced item, he could afford to sell the caviar at a loss.

34. Because Mr. Luxe was the owner of the store, he made the decisions on how to reduce theft.

35. Mr. Luxe's cheese clerk was absent from work for two months because of a back operation. During that time, Mr. Luxe was the only salesperson in the store.

36. The cheese clerk, Andy, increased the amount of caviar he stole each week.

37. Mr. Luxe felt that without packages to hide the caviar tins, thieves could not steal as easily.

38. Mr. Luxe had a door in his storeroom which the previous owner of the store had the key to.

39. Because Mr. Luxe did not check the orders he received, he was not aware that he had been billed for 20 cases of caviar but had received only 14.

40. The Russian caviar was a synthetic product made from gelatin.

SCORING

To find your score, compare your responses on the Answer Sheet to those on the Scoring Key below. Give yourself 1 point for each correct answer and write your total in the box below. You may wish to read the Explanatory Answers to help pinpoint any mistakes you have made.

TOTAL
SCORE

SCORING KEY

1.	d	14.	e	28.	c
2.	b	15.	c	29.	a
3.	e	16.	d	30.	e
4.	a	17.	d	31.	a
5.	c	18.	a	32.	e
6.	a	19.	d	33.	a
7.	d	20.	c	34.	c
8.	b	21.	e	35.	d
9.	c	22.	d	36.	b
10.	e	23.	b	37.	c
11.	a	24.	d	38.	d
12.	e	25.	d	39.	b
13.	b	26.	a	40.	e
		27.	b		

INTERPRETATION

You were presented with four situations and a result that came out of each. As you noticed, the result was occasionally an unexpected one, forcing you to use logical processes different from those you typically use.

Psychological research has shown that this type of skill involves what has been called a *field-independent* cognitive style. The field-independent person is able to differentiate objects from the context in which they are imbedded — a finding-a-needle-in-a-haystack analytical skill. On the other hand, the *field-dependent* person's perception is strongly dominated by the overall context, and it is often difficult for that person to separate the significant parts or information from the irrelevant material.

The norms for the Analysis-of-Explanations Test are as follows:

Strong performance:	30-40
Average performance:	20-29
Weak performance:	1-19

A strong performance on this test demonstrates the ability to separate information into the relevant and the irrelevant and to make decisions based on available data. This skill is an important one in fields where one must grasp a large amount of information and make effective decisions based on that data. Occupations involving management decisions in business, case planning in law, and new-product development in industry rely on such skills.

A low score on the test may mean that your strength is in making decisions in a formulaic fashion, moving from x to y to z. This type of problem-solving process is often found in technical and clerical occupations rather than those requiring analytical skills. Combine your performance here with those on other logic-related tests (such as Test 13, the Analytical Abilities Test) to get an idea of your overall analytical aptitude.

1. (d). The price of soybeans is relevant to an explanation of the closing of the farms based on the argument that soybeans could not be marketed successfully. This statement weakens such a plausible explanation.

2. (b). If the soil were permanently infertile, the farmers would have to close their farms for good. This is a possible explanation.

3. (e). Since the farmers were no longer planting wheat, this statement is irrelevant to a possible explanation of the closing of the farms.

4. (a). The farmers planted soybeans as the agronomist had recommended. Therefore this statement is inconsistent with the information given.

5. (c). This is clearly deducible from the agronomist's recommendation that soybeans, which would replenish the soil, be planted instead of wheat.

6. (a). From the result we know that there were only 50 farm families in Steep Valley. From the first sentence of the fact-situation we know that there were fewer than 100 families living in the valley (if 50 is more than half of the community there must be fewer than 100 altogether). Thus the number 600 is inconsistent.

7. (d). This is relevant to a possible explanation. If the farmers did not have five times as much water available as they had previously used for the wheat, this would explain why they may have lost their entire soybean crop. Such a loss could explain why the farmers had to close their farms.

8. (b). If the community were underwater, the farmers would have had to close their farms for good. This is a possible and plausible explanation.

9. (c). For a farming community which has long been dependent upon wheat to switch abruptly to soybeans indicates a willingness to take drastic measures to stay in business. Therefore, this statement is deducible.

10. (e). The reputation of Steep Valley wheat is irrelevant to an explanation for the closing of the farms three years later.

11. (a). Inconsistent. The passage states that Ruby Falls is in New York. It is, therefore, a northern, not a southern, school.

12. (e). Irrelevant. The level of academic excellence of Clover Canyon implied in this statement has no bearing on the issue at hand.

13. (b). This is an adequate explanation of the result because, as the name implies, a governing board governs the school. If the governing board was opposed to the idea of admitting men, the school would have little chance of becoming coed.

14. (e). The weather in South Carolina in 1966 is totally irrelevant.

15. (c). This statement is deducible since this is the means the financial board chose to raise additional funds.

16. (d). This statement would support a possible explanation of the result. It is not an adequate explanation, however, because student opinion alone does not necessarily dictate college policy.

17. (d). This strengthens the result but is not an adequate explanation by itself because we are not told how much money was needed to alleviate Clover Canyon's financial difficulties.

18. (a). Inconsistent. The passage states that most of the students were from South Carolina.

19. (d). The action of Daisy Hill could serve to weaken a possible argument that Clover Canyon did not become a coeducational institution because of lack of precedent in the South or of southern conservatism.

20. (c). This statement is deducible from the fact that the board voted unanimously in favor of admitting men.

21. (e). The topic of Ms. Moneybright's college thesis is irrelevant to her decision to switch jobs.

22. (d). Even though Ms. Moneybright was already making a great deal of money, a substantial raise is relevant to her decision to leave Dollars & Bills and might strengthen an argument that Dollars & Bills made an offer which Ms. Moneybright preferred to that of *The Financial Wizard*.

23. (b). If *The Financial Wizard* went out of business, Ms. Moneybright could not accept the new job and would remain in the employ of Dollars & Bills.

24. (d). A love affair with the president of the firm might induce Ms. Moneybright to change her decision to leave Dollars & Bills. Therefore the statement is relevant to a possible plausible explanation of the result. Note that falling in love with the president of Dollars & Bills, though relevant to an explanation, is not an adequate explanation in itself.

25. (d). Such a legal suit and the nature of such controversial articles may be relevant to Ms. Moneybright's decision to stay at Dollars & Bills.

26. (a). Ms. Moneybright held a B.A. in American literature and could not possibly be functionally illiterate.

27. (b). If *The Financial Wizard* were sold to Dollars & Bills, then Ms. Moneybright could have accepted the new job on *The Financial Wizard* and still be an employee of Dollars & Bills.

28. (c). This is deducible from Ms. Moneybright's background and the job offer from *The Financial Wizard*.

29. (a). Ms. Moneybright was dissatisfied with her job as a broker even though she made a great deal of money. Thus money is not Ms. Moneybright's only goal in working and the statement is inconsistent.

30. (e). This statement may in fact be true. The kind of editorial work Ms. Moneybright was offered does not necessarily require typing and she may have done all her writing in longhand. Ms. Moneybright's ability or inability to type is irrelevant to any explanation of why she remained in the employ of Dollars & Bills.

31. (a). Inconsistent. In the passage we learn that four cases of caviar had been stolen. The result states that six cases had been stolen. This is an increase in the theft rate.

32. (e). Irrelevant. It does not matter how many jars of caviar there were in each case because Mr. Luxe counted his caviar by the case.

33. (a). Inconsistent. The passage states that caviar was the highest-priced item.

34. (c). Deducible. The passage states that Mr. Luxe is the owner and describes the changes he implemented.

35. (d). This statement strengthens a possible explanation of the result because we know that the cheese clerk was supposed to have distributed the caviar. However, it is likely that Mr. Luxe would have taken measures to compensate for the clerk's absence. Therefore, the statement cannot stand by itself as an adequate explanation of the result.

36. (b). A possible explanation of the result. If Andy were stealing the caviar all along, as the statement implies, and if he increased his rate of theft, this would adequately account for the additional missing caviar.

37. (c). Deducible. If Mr. Luxe did not feel that the precaution would discourage potential thieves, he would not have instigated it.

38. (d). This statement strengthens a possible explanation of the result. The previous owner could have been entering at night and stealing caviar. Because there is no proof, however, that the previous owner was stealing the caviar, this statement is not an adequate explanation of the result.

39. (b). If Mr. Luxe had only received 14 cases of caviar instead of the 20 he thought he had received, it would seem as though 6 cases had been stolen when he went over his stock and books. This is an adequate explanation.

40. (e). The fact that the Russian caviar was made from gelatin is totally irrelevant.

4. Formal Operations Test

by William M. Bart

One of psychology's most significant theories was developed by Jean Piaget, a Swiss developmental psychologist who rode his bicycle to the university almost every working day until he died in 1980. Piaget's theory is concerned with cognitive development, those growth processes related to how we think and the ways in which we solve problems.

"Why is it," he wondered, "that a five-year-old thinks a tall, narrow glass contains more milk than a short but very wide glass, even when the child sees the milk poured from one glass to another and back again?" The answer, he found, is that the five-year-old has not yet developed the cognitive skills of *conservation* and *reversibility*. Such skills, according to Piaget, are the result of the interaction of the child's biological makeup with the environment and are part of the maturing process.

Piaget suggested that we grow through four distinct stages of cognitive development. Since the infant learns primarily from sensory stimulation, Piaget called the first stage *sensorimotor*. Children around age two enter the *preoperational stage*, during which they acquire language and the ability to think symbolically. From age seven to eleven or so the child develops the skills of conservation and reversibility; this is called the *concrete operations stage*. The fourth stage, theoretically the highest level of cognitive development, Piaget labeled *formal operations*. Here the individual is able to consider all of the possible relationships in problematic situations and also shows the capacity to think in a hypothetical "What if?" manner.

Supported by a combination of federal and university grants, Professor William Bart, of the University of Minnesota, developed a series of three tests to measure formal operational thought. The format and goals of all three tests are identical, though the content varies from biology, to literature, to history. Dr. Bart specified that each test item had to meet four criteria that you may find interesting before you take the test: (1) each premise in an item is either imaginary or absurd (contrary to fact); (2) in each item there are logical connections in the premises; (3) the task requires a simple deduction through the use of logical rules of inference; and (4) all premises in each item are assumed to be true. We have selected the biology test for you. Although the test items deal with biological terms, it is not necessary for you to be well versed in biology in order to do well on the test.

INSTRUCTIONS

In the Formal Operations Test you will be presented with 30 items. Each item consists of one premise or more followed by six possible conclusions. You are to assume that the premise is true, even if it is foreign to you or contrary to your experience. Determine which of the six conclusions is true and valid given that the premise is true.

Before you begin the test, remove the Answer Sheet on the next page and use it to record your responses. Give yourself 40 minutes to complete the test. When your time is up, stop your work and turn the page to find your score.

ANSWER SHEET

4. Formal Operations Test

	a	b	c	d	e	f		a	b	c	d	e	f
1.	0	0	0	0	0	0	16.	0	0	0	0	0	0
2.	0	0	0	0	0	0	17.	0	0	0	0	0	0
3.	0	0	0	0	0	0	18.	0	0	0	0	0	0
4.	0	0	0	0	0	0	19.	0	0	0	0	0	0
5.	0	0	0	0	0	0	20.	0	0	0	0	0	0
6.	0	0	0	0	0	0	21.	0	0	0	0	0	0
7.	0	0	0	0	0	0	22.	0	0	0	0	0	0
8.	0	0	0	0	0	0	23.	0	0	0	0	0	0
9.	0	0	0	0	0	0	24.	0	0	0	0	0	0
10.	0	0	0	0	0	0	25.	0	0	0	0	0	0
11.	0	0	0	0	0	0	26.	0	0	0	0	0	0
12.	0	0	0	0	0	0	27.	0	0	0	0	0	0
13.	0	0	0	0	0	0	28.	0	0	0	0	0	0
14.	0	0	0	0	0	0	29.	0	0	0	0	0	0
15.	0	0	0	0	0	0	30.	0	0	0	0	0	0

NOTES

(Tear Out)

ANSWER SHEET

4. Formal Operations Test

	a	b	c	d	e	f			a	b	c	d	e	f
1.	0	0	0	0	0	0		16.	0	0	0	0	0	0
2.	0	0	0	0	0	0		17.	0	0	0	0	0	0
3.	0	0	0	0	0	0		18.	0	0	0	0	0	0
4.	0	0	0	0	0	0		19.	0	0	0	0	0	0
5.	0	0	0	0	0	0		20.	0	0	0	0	0	0
6.	0	0	0	0	0	0		21.	0	0	0	0	0	0
7.	0	0	0	0	0	0		22.	0	0	0	0	0	0
8.	0	0	0	0	0	0		23.	0	0	0	0	0	0
9.	0	0	0	0	0	0		24.	0	0	0	0	0	0
10.	0	0	0	0	0	0		25.	0	0	0	0	0	0
11.	0	0	0	0	0	0		26.	0	0	0	0	0	0
12.	0	0	0	0	0	0		27.	0	0	0	0	0	0
13.	0	0	0	0	0	0		28.	0	0	0	0	0	0
14.	0	0	0	0	0	0		29.	0	0	0	0	0	0
15.	0	0	0	0	0	0		30.	0	0	0	0	0	0

NOTES

(Tear Out)

1. Either auxins are proteins or petioles grow on auxins. If auxins are proteins then petioles grow on auxins. Therefore:
   (a) Petioles grow on auxins.
   (b) Either auxins are not proteins or petioles do not grow on auxins.
   (c) If petioles grow on auxins then auxins are proteins.
   (d) Auxins are not proteins.
   (e) Auxins are petioles.
   (f) Auxins are proteins and petioles do not grow on auxins.

2. Whelks are more colorful than periwinkles. Whelks are less colorful than abalones. Therefore:
   (a) Whelks are the most colorful of the three animals.
   (b) Periwinkles are more colorful than abalones.
   (c) Periwinkles are the least colorful of the three animals.
   (d) Periwinkles are the most colorful of the three animals.
   (e) Abalones are the least colorful of the three animals.
   (f) Whelks are the least colorful of the three animals.

3. Worms move slower than lice and worms are smaller than mice. Worms move faster than mice and worms are larger than lice. Therefore:
   (a) Worms move the fastest and are the largest of the three animals.
   (b) Mice move faster than lice.
   (c) Mice are smaller than lice.
   (d) Lice move the fastest and are the largest of the three animals.
   (e) Lice move the fastest and are the smallest of the three animals.
   (f) Mice move the fastest and are the largest of the three animals.

4. No individual is a tapir. Therefore:
   (a) All individuals are not tapirs.
   (b) All individuals are tapirs and monkeys.
   (c) No individuals are tapirs.
   (d) All individuals are tapirs.
   (e) No individuals are not tapirs.
   (f) Some individuals are tapirs.

5. Either birch thrive or sage die. Birch do not thrive. Therefore:
   (a) Birch thrive if and only if sage die.
   (b) Sage do not die.
   (c) If sage die then birch thrive.
   (d) Birch thrive and sage die.
   (e) Sage die.
   (f) Birch thrive and sage do not die.

6. If amnions are red the chick embryos shrink. Amnions are not red and chick embryos shrink. Therefore:
   (a) If chick embryos shrink then amnions are red.
   (b) Amnions are red.
   (c) Amnions are red and chick embryos shrink.
   (d) Chick embryos do not shrink.
   (e) Amnions are red and chick embryos do not shrink.
   (f) Amnions are not red.

7. Manatees are reptiles if and only if lemurs are birds. Therefore:
   (a) If manatees are reptiles then lemurs are birds.
   (b) Manatees are not reptiles and lemurs are birds.
   (c) Manatees are reptiles and lemurs are not birds.
   (d) Manatees are reptiles.
   (e) Manatees are not reptiles.
   (f) Lemurs are birds.

8. Pink rays are not carnivores. Therefore:
   (a) If pink rays are carnivores then remoras ride on pink rays.
   (b) Pink rays are carnivores.
   (c) Remoras ride on pink rays.
   (d) Pink rays are carnivores and remoras do not ride on pink rays.
   (e) Pink rays are carnivores and remoras ride on pink rays.
   (f) Either pink rays are carnivores or remoras ride on pink rays.

9. All individuals are neither zebras nor rotifers. Therefore:
   (a) All individuals are zebras.
   (b) All individuals are rotifers.
   (c) All zebras are rotifers.
   (d) No individuals are zebras.
   (e) Some individuals are zebras.
   (f) All individuals are not zebras and rotifers.

10. Either tropisms occur in apes or taxes occur in bees. Tropisms occur in apes and taxes occur in bees. Therefore:
    (a) Taxes do not occur in bees.
    (b) Tropisms occur in apes and taxes do not occur in bees.
    (c) Tropisms occur in apes.
    (d) If tropisms occur in apes then taxes do not occur in bees.
    (e) Tropisms do not occur in apes.
    (f) Either tropisms do not occur in apes or taxes do not occur in bees.

11. All dace are platy. Some dace are cod. Therefore:
    (a) All cod are not platy.
    (b) Some cod are not platy.
    (c) Some cod are platy.
    (d) All platy are dace.
    (e) All dace are not cod.
    (f) Some dace are not cod.

12. Some skinks are plastrons. All turtles are not skinks. Therefore:
    (a) All skinks are not plastrons.
    (b) Some turtles are skinks.
    (c) All turtles are plastrons.
    (d) Some turtles are not plastrons.
    (e) Some skinks are not plastrons.
    (f) All skinks are turtles.

13. If wasps eat haploids then fly pupae are lost. Wasps do not eat haploids and fly pupae are not lost. Therefore:
    (a) Wasps eat haploids.
    (b) Either wasps eat haploids or fly pupae are lost.
    (c) Fly pupae are lost.
    (d) Fly pupae are not lost.
    (e) Wasps eat haploids and fly pupae are lost.
    (f) Wasps eat haploids and fly pupae are not lost.

14. All axolotls are bream. All catfish are not bream. Therefore:
    (a) All catfish are not axolotls.
    (b) Some axolotls are not bream.
    (c) Some catfish are bream.
    (d) All axolotls are not bream.
    (e) All bream are axolotls.
    (f) All bream are catfish.

15. Some peepers are killifish. All peepers are haddock. Therefore:
    (a) Some haddock are killifish.
    (b) All haddock are not killifish.
    (c) Some haddock are not killifish.
    (d) All haddock are peepers.
    (e) All peepers are killifish.
    (f) Some peepers are not haddock.

16. All blue wombats are skates. All skates are not nymphs. Therefore:
    (a) All nymphs are blue wombats.
    (b) Some nymphs are blue wombats.
    (c) All nymphs are not blue wombats.
    (d) Some blue wombats are not skates.
    (e) All skates are blue wombats.
    (f) Some skates are nymphs.

17. Either genes grow or dodders thrive. Genes do not grow and dodders thrive. Therefore:
    (a) Genes grow if and only if dodders thrive.
    (b) Genes grow and dodders thrive.
    (c) Genes grow.
    (d) If dodders thrive then genes grow.
    (e) Genes do not grow.
    (f) Genes do not grow and dodders do not thrive.

18. All medaka are sea horses. All orangefish are medaka. Therefore:
    (a) All medaka are not orangefish.
    (b) All orangefish are sea horses.
    (c) Some medaka are not sea horses.
    (d) Some orangefish are not medaka.
    (e) All medaka are not sea horses.
    (f) Some orangefish are not sea horses.

19. Margays are less aquatic than ocelots. Margays are more aquatic than penquins. Pike are less aquatic than penquins. Therefore:
    (a) Margays are the least aquatic of the four animals.
    (b) Pike are the most aquatic of the four animals.
    (c) Penquins are more aquatic than ocelots.
    (d) Ocelots are the most aquatic of the four animals.
    (e) Margays are the most aquatic of the four animals.
    (f) Penquins are the most aquatic of the four animals.

20. If water dissolves fat then acetone dissolves protein. Water dissolves fat if and only if acetone dissolves protein. Therefore:
    (a) Either water dissolves fat or acetone dissolves protein.
    (b) Water dissolves fat.
    (c) Acetone dissolves protein.
    (d) Water does not dissolve fat.
    (e) Acetone does not dissolve protein.
    (f) If water does not dissolve fat then acetone does not dissolve protein.

21. All ashes are not poplars. All locusts are ashes. Therefore:
    (a) All locusts are not ashes.
    (b) All ashes are poplars.
    (c) All locusts are poplars.
    (d) Some ashes are poplars.
    (e) Some locusts are not ashes.
    (f) All locusts are not poplars.

22. If yeast rises then caustic potash is present and if mold grows then limewater is present. Either caustic potash is not present or limewater is not present. Therefore:
    (a) Yeast does not rise.
    (b) Limewater is not present.
    (c) Either yeast does not rise or mold does not grow.
    (d) Limewater is present.
    (e) Yeast rises.
    (f) Yeast rises and limewater is present.

23. Some antigens are serums. All serums are donors. Therefore:
    (a) All donors are not antigens.
    (b) All donors are serums.
    (c) Some donors are not antigens.
    (d) All antigens are not serums.
    (e) Some donors are antigens.
    (f) Some donors are not serums.

24. If the Hardy-Weinberg law holds then Darwinian theory is false. If Darwinian theory is false then man is a naked ape. Therefore:
    (a) The Hardy-Weinberg law holds and Darwinian theory is false.
    (b) The Hardy-Weinberg law holds.
    (c) Darwinian theory is not false.
    (d) The Hardy-Weinberg law does not hold.
    (e) If the Hardy-Weinberg law holds then man is a naked ape.
    (f) Either the Hardy-Weinberg law holds or man is a naked ape.

25. If opah live in the Indian Ocean then bass live in the Black Sea and if gar thrive in Lake Chad then beavers live near Lake Chad. Either opah live in the Indian Ocean or gar thrive in Lake Chad. Therefore:
    (a) Bass live in the Black Sea and beavers live near Lake Chad.
    (b) Bass live in the Black Sea and gar thrive in Lake Chad.
    (c) Bass do not live in the Black Sea.
    (d) Beavers do not live near Lake Chad.
    (e) Beavers live near Lake Chad.
    (f) Either bass live in the Black Sea or beavers live near Lake Chad.

26. Sycamores are smaller than red elms. Sycamores are larger than sequoias. Therefore:
    (a) Sycamores are the largest of the three trees.
    (b) Red elms are the largest of the three trees.
    (c) Sequoias are larger than red elms.
    (d) Red elms are the smallest of the three trees.
    (e) Sycamores are the smallest of the three trees.
    (f) Sequoias are the largest of the three trees.

27. Chordates are less numerous than crustaceans. Mollusks are more numerous than crustaceans. Mollusks are less numerous than ciliates. Therefore:
    (a) Chordates are the least numerous of the four animals.
    (b) Ciliates are less numerous than crustaceans.
    (c) Chordates are more numerous than mollusks.
    (d) Ciliates are the least numerous of the four animals.
    (e) Mollusks are the least numerous of the four animals.
    (f) Mollusks are the most numerous of the four animals.

28. Either flagellates grow in ice or sponges reproduce in icy water. Therefore:
    (a) Flagellates do not grow in ice.
    (b) Flagellates do not grow in ice and sponges reproduce in icy water.
    (c) Sponges reproduce in icy water.
    (d) If flagellates do not grow in ice then sponges reproduce in icy water.
    (e) Flagellates grow in ice.
    (f) If flagellates grow in ice then sponges reproduce in icy water.

29. All blue monocots are parsnips. Therefore:
    (a) If all individuals are blue then all monocots are parsnips.
    (b) All individuals are blue.
    (c) All individuals are blue monocot parsnips.
    (d) All individuals are monocots.
    (e) All individuals are either blue or monocots.
    (f) All individuals are parsnips.

30. Oaks are not fungi if and only if oats are flowers. Therefore:
    (a) If oaks are fungi then oats are not flowers.
    (b) Oaks are not fungi and oats are not flowers.
    (c) Oaks are fungi and oats are not flowers.
    (d) Oaks are fungi.
    (e) Oaks are not fungi.
    (f) Oats are flowers.

SCORING

To find your score, compare your responses on the Answer Sheet to those on the Scoring Key below. Give yourself 1 point for each correct answer and write the total in the box below.

TOTAL SCORE

SCORING KEY

1.	a	16.	c
2.	c	17.	e
3.	e	18.	b
4.	a	19.	d
5.	e	20.	f
6.	f	21.	f
7.	a	22.	c
8.	a	23.	e
9.	f	24.	e
10.	c	25.	f
11.	c	26.	b
12.	d	27.	a
13.	d	28.	d
14.	a	29.	a
15.	a	30.	a

INTERPRETATION

Many components of intellect (such as vocabulary size) increase as we get older. Piaget theorized, however, that formal reasoning becomes well established in a relatively short period of time after its emergence — if it emerges at all. Some psychologists using Piaget's rigorous definition of formal operational thought have speculated that perhaps less than one half of all adults ever develop true formal-reasoning ability.

Professor Bart found that two people out of three in his adult norm group scored between 15 and 24 on the Formal Operations Test in Biology. A score below 15 thus represents a weak performance on this test of formal operational thought. If you scored here, it's not likely that being rushed by the time limit was the problem, though you may have responded to the time limit by feeling pressured to answer quickly. A low score does suggest that you might be happier and more effective in jobs that require less formal-reasoning skill — production work instead of management, office work rather than administration.

Scores between 15 and 24 represent the range in which most people score. Such a score most likely means that you enjoy playing with logical problems in order to produce the best results. Increased practice of tasks requiring such abstract thought can help your formal reasoning skills.

If you scored above 24 on the Formal Operations Test, the questions were probably a lot of fun for you. And you probably disagreed with the keyed answers for the ones you missed. You should take pride in your reasoning skills. A high level of formal reasoning ability allows you to formulate hypotheses and design ways to check potential solutions. Such skills are essential in occupations involving research and problem analysis. Political science, law, mathematics, emergency medicine, and mystery writing all require high levels of this ability.

5. General Mathematics Test

A primary component of all general intelligence measures is mathematical understanding and skill in applying math concepts. Mathematical abilities are also heavily weighted in tests that predict success in graduate school, particularly for fields that rely on quantitative skills, such as accounting, engineering, and the sciences.

The questions that follow measure aptitude in general mathematics, simple algebra, and geometry. They involve reasoning about quantitative relationships more than they test arithmetic fundamentals. That does not mean, however, that basic arithmetic knowledge isn't necessary to do well on the test. The questions assume a basic knowledge of math and go on to emphasize the comprehension of numerical concepts and the application of mathematical principles to problem-solving. They will test the extent and depth of your quantitative understanding and your ability to apply that knowledge.

INSTRUCTIONS

In the General Mathematics Test, which begins below, you will be given 25 problems with multiple-choice answers. Select the choice that best answers the question or completes the statement.

Before you begin the test, turn the page and tear out the Answer Sheet. There is space on the Answer Sheet for computing your responses. Give yourself 30 minutes to complete the test. When your time is up, stop your work and turn the page to find your score.

© 1980 Arco Publishing, Inc. From The Graduate Record Examination Aptitude Test by the Arco Editorial Board.

1. In 2 hours, the minute hand of a clock rotates through an angle of
    (a) 60°
    (b) 90°
    (c) 180°
    (d) 360°
    (e) 720°

2. Which of the following fractions is less than ⅓?
    (a) $22/63$
    (b) $4/11$
    (c) $15/46$
    (d) $33/98$
    (e) $102/303$

3. The length of each side of the square below is $\frac{2x}{3} + 1$. The perimeter of the square is

    (a) $\frac{8x + 4}{3}$

    (b) $\frac{8x + 12}{3}$

    (c) $\frac{2x}{3} + 4$

    (d) $\frac{2x}{3} + 16$

    (e) $\frac{4x}{3} + 2$

    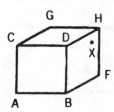

4. An individual intelligence test is administered to John A when he is 10 years, 8 months old. His recorded MA (mental age) is 160 months. What IQ should be recorded?
    (a) 80
    (b) 125
    (c) 128
    (d) 148
    (e) 160

5. When it is noon at prime meridian on the equator, what time is it at 75° north latitude on this meridian?
    (a) 12 noon
    (b) 3 P.M.
    (c) 5 P.M.
    (d) 7 A.M.
    (e) midnight

QUESTIONS 6 THROUGH 9 ARE TO BE ANSWERED WITH REFERENCE TO THE FOLLOWING DIAGRAM:

The diagram shows a cube. Each corner has been identified by a letter. Corner E is not shown, but its location is the one corner not shown in the diagram. The cube has a 1-inch side.

6. The distance from A to D is
    (a) 1 inch
    (b) 2 inches
    (c) $\sqrt{2}$ inches
    (d) $\sqrt{3}$ inches
    (e) $\frac{1}{\sqrt{2}}$ inches

7. There is a dot X on the BDHF face of the cube. If we let the cube rotate 180° in a clockwise direction on an axis running through A and H, the
    (a) cube will be standing on corner C
    (b) dot X will appear in the plane where face ABDC is now shown
    (c) dot X will be in the plane where face CDHG is now shown
    (d) cube will return to its position as shown in the diagram
    (e) corner C will appear in the place where corner F is now shown

8. The distance from A to X is
    (a) more than 2 inches
    (b) less than 1 inch
    (c) between 1 and $\sqrt{3}$ inches
    (d) between $\sqrt{3}$ and 2 inches
    (e) exactly $\sqrt{3}$ inches

9. If the cube is successively rotated 180° on axes going through the center of faces ABDC and EFHG, faces AEGC and BDHF, and faces CDHG and ABEF, where will the face containing point X be?
    (a) where face BDHF was at the start of the operation
    (b) where face AEGC was at the start of the operation
    (c) where face EFHG was at the start of the operation
    (d) where face ABFE was at the start of the operation
    (e) where face ABDC was at the start of the operation

10. A carpenter needs four boards, each 2 feet, 9 inches long. If wood is sold only by the foot, how many feet must he buy?
    (a) 9
    (b) 10
    (c) 11
    (d) 12
    (e) 13

11. CMXLIX in Roman numerals is the equivalent of
    (a) 449
    (b) 949
    (c) 969
    (d) 1,149
    (e) 1,169

QUESTIONS 12 THROUGH 16 ARE TO BE ANSWERED WITH REFERENCE TO THE ADJOINING GRAPH:

12. The period with the smallest increase in total passenger-miles was
    (a) 1951–1952
    (b) 1954–1955
    (c) 1955–1956
    (d) 1957–1958
    (e) 1958–1959

13. Which statement is *not* true?
    (a) Excluding 1960, there were more deaths in the aggregate, per 100 million passenger-miles, during the odd years than during the even years.
    (b) There was an increase in passenger-miles flown from 1950 to 1957.
    (c) There has been an increase in passenger-deaths every year since 1950.
    (d) There were more passenger-deaths in 1960 than 1950.
    (e) Thirty billion passenger-miles were flown in 1959.

48

ANSWER SHEET

5. General Mathematics Test

	a	b	c	d	e		a	b	c	d	e
1.	0	0	0	0	0	14.	0	0	0	0	0
2.	0	0	0	0	0	15.	0	0	0	0	0
3.	0	0	0	0	0	16.	0	0	0	0	0
4.	0	0	0	0	0	17.	0	0	0	0	0
5.	0	0	0	0	0	18.	0	0	0	0	0
6.	0	0	0	0	0	19.	0	0	0	0	0
7.	0	0	0	0	0	20.	0	0	0	0	0
8.	0	0	0	0	0	21.	0	0	0	0	0
9.	0	0	0	0	0	22.	0	0	0	0	0
10.	0	0	0	0	0	23.	0	0	0	0	0
11.	0	0	0	0	0	24.	0	0	0	0	0
12.	0	0	0	0	0	25.	0	0	0	0	0
13.	0	0	0	0	0						

NOTES

(Tear Out)

ANSWER SHEET

5. General Mathematics Test

	a	b	c	d	e		a	b	c	d	e
1.	0	0	0	0	0	14.	0	0	0	0	0
2.	0	0	0	0	0	15.	0	0	0	0	0
3.	0	0	0	0	0	16.	0	0	0	0	0
4.	0	0	0	0	0	17.	0	0	0	0	0
5.	0	0	0	0	0	18.	0	0	0	0	0
6.	0	0	0	0	0	19.	0	0	0	0	0
7.	0	0	0	0	0	20.	0	0	0	0	0
8.	0	0	0	0	0	21.	0	0	0	0	0
9.	0	0	0	0	0	22.	0	0	0	0	0
10.	0	0	0	0	0	23.	0	0	0	0	0
11.	0	0	0	0	0	24.	0	0	0	0	0
12.	0	0	0	0	0	25.	0	0	0	0	0
13.	0	0	0	0	0						

NOTES

14. The greatest and the least number of passenger-deaths occurred during
    (a) 1950 and 1957
    (b) 1954 and 1960
    (c) 1952 and 1955
    (d) 1953 and 1956
    (e) 1954 and 1957

15. In 1955, passenger-deaths numbered approximately
    (a) 24
    (b) 240
    (c) 2,400
    (d) 24,000
    (e) 240,000

16. The sharpest drop in passenger-deaths per 100 million miles was during the period of
    (a) 1951–1952
    (b) 1953–1954
    (c) 1954–1955
    (d) 1955–1956
    (e) 1957–1958

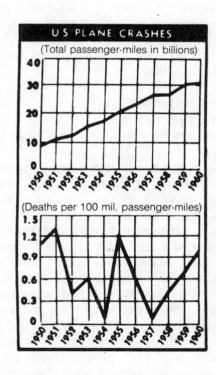

US PLANE CRASHES

(Total passenger-miles in billions)

(Deaths per 100 mil. passenger-miles)

QUESTIONS 17 THROUGH 21 ARE TO BE ANSWERED WITH REFERENCE TO THE FOLLOWING PARAGRAPH:

Five geometric figures have been drawn: an isosceles triangle with base equal to its altitude = *a*, a square with side = *a*, a circle with a radius = *a*, a regular hexagon with each side = *a*, and a semicircle with a diameter = *a*. (The figures are not drawn to scale. All the questions assume the stated dimensions.)

17. Which figure has the greatest area?
    (a) △
    (b) □
    (c) ○
    (d) ⬡
    (e) ◠

18. Which figure has the smallest perimeter?
    (a) □
    (b) △
    (c) ○
    (d) ⬡
    (e) ◠

19. Which of the following statements is true?
    (a) ○ can be inscribed inside □ .
    (b) □ can be inscribed inside △ .
    (c) ⬡ can be inscribed inside □ .
    (d) ⬡ can be inscribed inside ○ .
    (e) △ can be inscribed inside ◠ .

20. Which of these statements is true? The area of
    (a) △ is just ⅙ the area of ⬡
    (b) △ is just ½ the area of □
    (c) □ is just ½ the area of ⬡
    (d) ⬡ is just ¾ the area of ○
    (e) ◠ is just ½ the area of ○

21. The ratio of the areas of ◠ and ○ is
    (a) 1:8
    (b) 1:6
    (c) 1:4
    (d) 1:2
    (e) 1:1

22. A motorist travels 120 miles to his destination at the average speed of 60 miles per hour and returns to the starting point at the average speed of 40 miles per hour. His average speed for the entire trip is
    (a) 53 miles per hour
    (b) 50 miles per hour
    (c) 48 miles per hour
    (d) 45 miles per hour
    (e) 52 miles per hour

23. A snapshot measures 2½ inches by 1⅞ inches. It is to be enlarged so that the longer dimension will be 4 inches. The length of the enlarged shorter dimension will be
    (a) 2½ inches
    (b) 3 inches
    (c) 3⅜ inches
    (d) 2⅝ inches
    (e) none of these

24. From a piece of tin the shape of a square 6 inches on a side, the largest possible circle is cut out. Of the following, the ratio of the area of the circle to the area of the original square is closest in value to
    (a) ⅘
    (b) ⅔
    (c) ⅗
    (d) ½
    (e) ¾

25. The approximate distance, *s*, in feet that an object falls in *t* seconds when dropped from a height is obtained by the use of the formula $s = 16t^2$. In 8 seconds the object will fall
    (a) 15,384 feet
    (b) 1,024 feet
    (c) 256 feet
    (d) 2,048 feet
    (e) none of these

SCORING

To score the test, compare your answers on the Answer Sheet to the Scoring Key below. Give yourself 1 point for each correct answer and write the total in the box below. For a discussion of the correct answers to the questions, see the Explanatory Answers.

TOTAL SCORE

SCORING KEY

1.	e	14.	b
2.	c	15.	b
3.	b	16.	a
4.	b	17.	c
5.	a	18.	e
6.	c	19.	d
7.	a	20.	b
8.	c	21.	a
9.	a	22.	c
10.	c	23.	b
11.	b	24.	a
12.	d	25.	b
13.	c		

INTERPRETATION

Your score on the General Mathematics Test will answer two basic questions: How well do you understand ideas expressed through numbers? How well can you think and analyze using numbers?

Mathematical (or numerical) skill is one of those abilities central to human survival. It is involved both in daily decisions and planning for the future. Educators regard the level of numerical skill as a way of predicting, to some extent, a student's success in school. In fact, the manual for the Psychological Corporation's Differential Aptitude Test battery states, "Numerical ability is one element of all-around ability to master academic work." The combination of mathematical ability and verbal reasoning is frequently seen as the best estimate of scholastic aptitude — the ability to perform well in most academic arenas.

Norms for the General Mathematics Test show the following ability groups:

Strong performance:	17-25
Average performance:	9-16
Weak performance:	1-8

As you interpret your own score, keep in mind not only how many questions you answered correctly but also which ones caused you the most difficulty. The questions on this test require, in addition to basic mathematical knowledge (the formula for the area of a circle, for example), reasoning abilities using numerical concepts. Thus errors could occur in either skill area. To gain the most from this test, you may want to examine the type of questions you missed in addition to computing your overall score.

If you scored high on this test, your performance is associated with success in such academic subjects as mathematics, physics, chemistry, and engineering. The test involves skills needed in many technical training programs as well. Numerical ability is useful in such occupations as laboratory research, business and manufacturing, computer programming, and accounting.

EXPLANATORY ANSWERS

1. **(e).** Every hour, the minute hand of a clock goes around once, or 360°. In 2 hours, it rotates 720°.

2. **(c).** $^{15}/_{45}$ would be ⅓. With a larger denominator, the fraction $^{15}/_{46}$ is less than ⅓.

3. **(b).** Since the perimeter of a square is 4 times the length of a side, it is
$$4\left(\frac{2x}{3} + 1\right), \text{ or } \frac{8x + 12}{3}$$

4. **(b).** IQ is 100 times this result: the mental age of a person divided by his chronological age. This is $100 \times 160 \div 128$, which equals 125.

5. **(a).** Time does not vary with latitude (distance from the equator), but only with longitude (distance from the prime meridian).

6. **(c).** ABD forms a right triangle with both legs equal to 1 inch. By the Pythagorean theorem, $AD = \sqrt{2}$.

7. **(a).** Imagine the triangle ACH rotated 180° about AH. C will be lower than the present position of the ABFE plane.

8. **(c).** AX must be shorter than AH, which is $\sqrt{3}$, and longer than AB, which is 1.

9. **(a).** The first rotation puts X where ACGE was. The second leaves X in the same plane. The third rotation returns X to its original position.

10. **(c).** The carpenter needs a total of 33 inches for each board. The total length is 132 inches, or 11 feet.

11. **(b).** CM equals $1000 - 100$, or 900.
XL equals $50 - 10$, or 40.
IX equals $10 - 1$, or 9.
Their sum is 949.

12. **(d).** The line in the top graph is almost horizontal between 1957 and 1958. In the other years, the line is rising.

13. **(c).** In 1955, there were 1.2 deaths per 100 million passenger-miles, and 20 billion passenger-miles, which means there were 240 deaths. In 1956, there were 0.6 deaths per 100 million passenger-miles, and about 24 billion passenger-miles, which means there were about 144 deaths.

14. **(b).** In 1954, there were only 18 deaths, and in 1960, there were 300.

15. **(b).** See calculations for number 13.

16. **(a).** In the period from 1951 to 1952, the death rate dropped to about one third of its previous level.

The answers to 17 through 21 can be readily seen from the diagram below.

17. **(c).**

18. **(e).**

19. **(d).**

20. **(b).**

21. **(a).**

22. **(c).** In the first trip, the motorist travels 120 miles at 60 m.p.h., which takes two hours. On the way back, he travels the same distance at 40 m.p.h., which takes three hours. His average rate is the total distance (240 miles) divided by the total time (5 hours), which yields 48 m.p.h.

23. **(b).** The proportion to be solved is $2\frac{1}{2}:4 = 1\frac{7}{8}:x$, where x is the length of the shorter dimension of the enlargement. Solving, $x = 3$.

24. **(a).** The area of the circle is π times the square of the radius, or 9π. The area of the square is 36. Thus, the ratio is $\frac{9\pi}{36}$, or $\frac{\pi}{4}$. Approximating π as 3.14, we divide and obtain .785, which is closest to $^4/_5$.

25. **(b).** By simple substitutions, $s = 16 \times 8 \times 8$, or 1,024.

6. Science Vocabulary Inventory

by Paul Bethume

One feature of the present decade is the popularization of science. Local newspapers feature scientific advances researched half a world away; national newsmagazines carry cover stories on genetic engineering; and popular TV talk shows treat science as an entertaining topic. But science has always emphasized its own jargon, a language of terms that to many of us seem to have been developed light-years away in another galaxy. Understanding such jargon, however, may become essential to our very survival — or at least to our ability to read about, understand, and use the sciences that affect our lives.

Two simultaneous studies conducted by Dr. Paul Bethume found a very large discrepancy between the scientific words students actually knew and vocabulary estimates by their instructors. Dr. Bethume's concerns were twofold: that comprehensive vocabulary tests had not been developed for scientific terms and that available tests did not "try to determine the depth of understanding," only the "measure of commonness of their vocabulary."

The Science Vocabulary Inventory is the result of his extensive research program. Over 3,000 students from 120 classes participated in the research that produced this inventory. Two hundred eighty-eight scientific terms were selected and divided into six tests of 48 items each. The test below is one of those.

INSTRUCTIONS

The Science Vocabulary Inventory contains six groups of scientific terms, with eight words and ten responses in each group. Each group is complete in itself, and descriptions of all eight words in a group are in that group's ten responses. Each numbered scientific term has one reasonable response. Choose the best response and write its letter in the space provided.

Give yourself four minutes to complete this test. When your time is up, stop your work and turn the page to find your score.

_____ 1. reverse	(a) part of an atom
_____ 2. proton	(b) height
_____ 3. ventricle	(c) slows down moving objects
_____ 4. friction	(d) has to do with sound
_____ 5. biennial	(e) once in two years
_____ 6. secretion	(f) something given off
_____ 7. acoustics	(g) go the other way
_____ 8. taxonomy	(h) part of the heart
	(j) balance
	(k) name system

_____ 9. techniques	(a) work against
_____ 10. endothermic	(b) methods of doing
_____ 11. anaerobic	(c) turn from a gas to a liquid
_____ 12. condense	(d) takes in heat
_____ 13. nucleus	(e) good tasting
_____ 14. compounds	(f) without air
_____ 15. formulas	(g) made up of more than one thing
_____ 16. resistance	(h) talk over
	(j) middle of an egg or atom
	(k) patterns for doing things

_____ 17. dissect	(a) sleep
_____ 18. distill	(b) change from a liquid to a gas to a liquid
_____ 19. narcosis	(c) picture
_____ 20. epidermis	(d) move back and forth
_____ 21. chlorophyll	(e) pulling away from the center
_____ 22. exothermic	(f) lying down
_____ 23. oscillation	(g) cut up
_____ 24. centrifugal	(h) gives off heat
	(j) green in plants
	(k) skin

_____ 25. trajectory	(a) know what something is
_____ 26. elastic	(b) won't flow
_____ 27. viscosity	(c) lead
_____ 28. conduct	(d) fill
_____ 29. identify	(e) moving forward
_____ 30. apparatus	(f) empty space
_____ 31. progressive	(g) things
_____ 32. vacuum	(h) change shape, then return to original shape
	(j) fall out
	(k) path

_____ 33. environment	(a) plant eaters
_____ 34. herbivores	(b) both halves the same
_____ 35. superpose	(c) can dissolve
_____ 36. symmetry	(d) symbol
_____ 37. generate	(e) start
_____ 38. soluble	(f) surroundings, where we live
_____ 39. abyss	(g) deep, without bottom
_____ 40. pressure	(h) one on top of another
	(j) something final
	(k) a force, a push

_____ 41. diet	(a) bend
_____ 42. rotate	(b) idea in the mind
_____ 43. cycle	(c) same thing, all the same
_____ 44. heterogeneous	(d) do damage to
_____ 45. refract	(e) different things
_____ 46. abstract	(f) special meals or food
_____ 47. uncertainty	(g) not sure
_____ 48. homogeneous	(h) tube or cavity
	(j) turn
	(k) circle of events

SCORING

9.	b
10.	d
11.	f
12.	c
13.	j
14.	g
15.	k
16.	a
17.	g
18.	b
19.	a
20.	k
21.	j
22.	h
23.	d
24.	e
25.	k
26.	h
27.	b
28.	c
29.	a
30.	g
31.	e
32.	f
33.	f
34.	a
35.	h
36.	b
37.	e
38.	c
39.	g
40.	k

1.	g	41.	f
2.	a	42.	j
3.	h	43.	k
4.	c	44.	e
5.	e	45.	a
6.	f	46.	b
7.	d	47.	g
8.	k	48.	c

FOLD BACK TO SCORE

To score the test, fold this page back on the dotted line and compare your answers to those on the Scoring Key. Give yourself 1 point for each correct answer.

☐

TOTAL
SCORE

INTERPRETATION

Although this section of the Science Vocabulary Inventory contains only 48 terms, a score of 43 or higher does suggest that you are very familiar with scientific language. You may have gained your knowledge from reading or from direct contact with science projects or academic training.

In addition to indicating above-average scientific vocabulary — the level needed for careers or avocations in science-related areas — your high score shows an effective linear approach to answering questions such as these. Your score may be due to partial knowledge of the correct answers combined with the ability to eliminate incorrect alternatives. Using such a process skillfully can add to limited knowledge in other context areas and is an important ability in its own right.

A score in the average range (34 to 42) would indicate that you've had some scientific training or are familiar with the scientific terms that appear with increasing frequency in the media. If you are not involved with the sciences but score in this range, your score reflects your ability to retain and apply information in this field and probably in others.

A low-to-average score of 33 or below may not strictly indicate a low level of scientific knowledge. Ask yourself if the speed aspect of the test affected your ability to concentrate. And did you give up if the words were not immediately known to you, rather than going through the process of eliminating those responses that you knew to be incorrect? If either of these factors affected you, then you might work on improving your strategies for such tests. Many good books are available that give you step-by-step guidelines for effective test-taking. Your score on this or any test is a combination of what you know and how well you've developed your test-taking techniques.

If, on the other hand, your score is low and accurately reflects your knowledge of scientific terms, you may want to broaden your knowledge by reading popular scientific magazines or books. Keeping abreast of science is becoming an important factor in understanding current events. Such knowledge can also provide you with useful information about yourself and about ways to improve your life.

7. Word Translation Test

"The hypothesis that ability in languages is really a bundle of many separate abilities, which has long been assumed by psychologists and modern language teachers, finds significant and detailed confirmation in these pages."

This statement is from the 1929 book *Prognosis Tests in Modern Foreign Languages*, written by the American and Canadian Committee on Foreign Languages. The book presents an analysis of research on predicting the likelihood of success in learning a new language. The tests in the book do not, however, measure the ability to learn French, for example. They are designed to gauge the special aptitudes that one must have if he or she wishes to become an intellectual convert — that is, to think in a language other than one's native tongue.

Therefore many of the tests use Esperanto — a language no one speaks. The original purpose of Esperanto was that of a universal language, one that would be taught in schools worldwide. It was hoped that such a universal tongue would simplify intergovernmental communication, directly increasing the likelihood of world peace.

As you take the test that follows, do not think of it as merely measuring your ability to learn a foreign language. It tests much more than that. The skills needed to do well on this test are related to many other areas. The linear skill that you need to go from paragraph to paragraph to question is basic to verbal intelligence.

INSTRUCTIONS

On the next page you will be presented with two paragraphs. The first will tell a story in English. In the second paragraph, the English story is translated into Esperanto. On the facing page is a series of English words. You will be asked to indicate their Esperanto equivalents, using information that you gained from the paragraphs. When the test begins, read both paragraphs through before answering the questions.

Give yourself ten minutes to complete the test. When your time is up, stop your work and turn the page to find your score.

A professor of zoology did not like it very much when his students were late at the beginning of his lecture, and at that time, interrupting his reading, he always expressed his annoyance to the tardy student. On one occasion, when the professor was reading about a horse, a certain tardy student entered the classroom. To the amazement of the students, contrary to his custom, the professor said nothing to the student and continued his reading. Finishing his reading about the horse, he said, *"Now,* gentlemen, after the horse let us turn to the donkey,'' and turning toward the latecomer, he said, ''I beg you sit down.'' ''Do not get excited, Mr. Professor,'' replied the student. ''I can listen to a donkey standing, too.''

Profesoro de zoologio tre ne amis, kiam la studentoj malfruis al la komenco de la lekcio kaj tiam, interrompante sian legadon, li ĉiam esprimadis sian malplezuron al la malfruinta studento. Un fojon, kiam la profesoro legis pri ĉevalo, eniris en la legejon iu malfruinta studento. Al la miro de la studentoj, kontrau sia kutimo la profesoro nenion diris al la studento kaj daurigis sian legadon. Fininte la legadon pri ĉevalo, li diris: — Nun, sinjoroj, post la ''ĉevalo'' ni transiru al la ''azeno,'' kaj, turninte sin al la malfruinta, li diris: Mi petas, sidiĝu. — Ne maltrankviligu vin, sinjoro profesoro, respondis la studento, mi povas auskulti azenon ankau starante.

Indicate the Esperanto equivalent for each of the following English words by writing the letter of the Esperanto in the space provided.

_____ 1. interrupting (a) legadon (b) esprimadis (c) daurigis (d) interrompante (e) sian

_____ 2. student (a) miro (b) studentoj (c) studento (d) sinjoro (e) malfruinta

_____ 3. reading (a) legadon (b) miro (c) fininte (d) ĉevalo (e) tre

_____ 4. and (a) al (b) la (c) sin (d) tiam (e) kaj

_____ 5. were late (a) komenco (b) malfruis (c) la (d) al (e) kiam

_____ 6. was reading (a) kiam (b) pri (c) eniris (d) legis (e) diris

_____ 7. professor (a) profesoro (b) post (c) legis (d) petas (e) zoologio

_____ 8. to (a) la (b) sin (c) malfruinta (d) al (e) de

_____ 9. nothing (a) ne (b) nenion (c) mi (d) kutimo (e) diris

_____ 10. gentlemen (a) studentoj (b) post (c) sidiĝu (d) profesoro (e) sinjoroj

_____ 11. sit down (a) petas (b) post la (c) sidiĝu (d) sin al (e) maltrankviligu

_____ 12. replied (a) esprimadis (b) respondis (c) malplezuron (d) sian (e) diris

_____ 13. standing (a) ankau (b) sian (c) starante (d) sinjoroj (e) azenon

_____ 14. his (a) sian (b) sin (c) ĉiam (d) kaj (e) legadon

_____ 15. the (a) al (b) li (c) sin (d) in (e) la

_____ 16. finishing (a) legadon (b) kontrau (c) turninte (d) fininte (e) nenion

_____ 17. turning (a) fininte (b) azeno (c) turninte (d) al (e) sin

_____ 18. beginning (a) komenco (b) malfruis (c) diris (d) interrompante (e) auskulti

_____ 19. about (a) ĉevalo (b) kiam (c) pri (d) post (e) ankau

_____ 20. of (a) la (b) al (c) li (d) en (e) de

_____ 21. tardy (a) malfruis (b) malfruinta (c) malplezuron (d) studento (e) turninte

_____ 22. said (a) nenion (b) studento (c) sian (d) sidiĝu (e) diris

_____ 23. after (a) la (b) kiam (c) ĉevalo (d) post (e) azeno

_____ 24. not (a) ne (b) mi (c) non (d) in (e) nun

_____ 25. I (a) ne (b) ni (c) in (d) mi (e) li

_____ 26. he (a) mi (b) li (c) la (d) sia (e) ĉiam

_____ 27. amazement (a) al (b) azenon (c) miro (d) kutimo (e) malplezuron

_____ 28. horse (a) diris (b) ĉevalo (c) azenon (d) legadon (e) daurigis

_____ 29. toward (a) sin (b) tiam (c) la (d) al (e) nenion

_____ 30. lecture (a) lekcio (b) legadon (c) studento (d) kutimo (e) komenco

59

1. d
2. c
3. a
4. e
5. b
6. d
7. a
8. d
9. b
10. e
11. c
12. b
13. c
14. a
15. e
16. d
17. c
18. a
19. c
20. e
21. b
22. e
23. d
24. a
25. d
26. b
27. c
28. b
29. a
30. a

FOLD BACK TO SCORE

SCORING

To score the test, fold this page on the dotted line and compare your answers to those on the Scoring Key. Give yourself 1 point for each correct answer and write the total in the box below.

TOTAL
SCORE

INTERPRETATION

The Word Translation Test (WTT) was developed to serve as a prognostic test, meaning a score can be used as a basis for advising someone to go into — or stay out of — foreign language programs. As its authors wrote in 1929, it was designed ''to present exercises in a new language which apply certain grammatical or syntactical rules either by translation or by the interpretation of syntax.'' The abilities required to score well on this test include basic problem-solving skills in the context of language translation.

A score of 24 to 30 on the WTT shows strong ability in the intellectual areas usually associated with the brain's left hemisphere — analytical and sequential information processing. These skills are important in many verbal areas, including the learning of a new language. The WTT requires you to transfer meanings of words in one paragraph to syntactically similar words in a second paragraph and a second language. Performing well on the WTT indicates more than the ease with which you may be able to learn a new language. It also suggests that you would do well in various analytical and problem-solving occupations — for example, business analysis, engineering, and systems analysis.

A score of 0 to 23 on the WTT is an excellent reason for you to continue on to the next chapter in *The Brain Game*, which features tests that measure predominantly right-hemisphere abilities. If your low score on the WTT is consistent with your performance on other tests in this chapter, then jobs emphasizing verbal and analytical skills may not be for you. Take those tests that measure such areas as spatial orientation or creative ability and plan your occupational strategy around your overall strengths and weaknesses.

Portrait of a Young Woman
Called Mlle. Charlotte du Val-d'Ognes
Artist Unknown
The Metropolitan Museum of Art
New York

CHAPTER TWO

THE RIGHT
HEMISPHERE

throughout our lives have been aimed at the brain's left-hemisphere abilities: language learning, mathematics, and formal logic. These tests are justified because they do tend to predict financial or academic success in a society such as ours. They do not, however, effectively measure such abilities as creativity, artistic skills, intuitive understanding, creative problem solving, or originality — all necessary skills for real intellectual achievement. These processes appear to occur in the right hemisphere of the brain.

The right hemisphere specializes in nonlinguistic, nonlinear functions. It has a superior capacity for comprehending complex visual and spatial relationships, and it seems to process information in a holistic fashion rather than sequentially or analytically. In other words, the right hemisphere appears to know more about the whole and leaves the classification of the parts to its counterpart on the left.

Scientists began to understand the distinct functions of the hemispheres by observing the behavior of persons who had suffered injuries to one hemisphere or the other. Those who sustain damage to the left side of the brain most often experience problems in speech, whereas those with right-hemisphere injuries experience perceptual problems. The latter include difficulties in spatial orientation and the ability to remember spatial relationships, skills required to learn one's way around, for instance, a large college campus. Persons with right-brain damage would also have a difficult time recognizing faces, although the ability to recall names might be largely unaffected.

As we increase our understanding of the functions of the human mind, we are beginning to appreciate the impact that these subtle right-hemisphere skills have on our intellectual development. The ability to perceive complex patterns and relationships that cannot be defined in mere words, and may not be logical in the formal sense, is vital for the intellectual growth of a secure, well-rounded, evolving society.

The tests that follow will measure your visual-spatial skills as well as your aesthetic abilities, imagination, and powers of observation. Even if your highest aptitudes do not lie in these areas, they are an important part of the creative process in any intellectual pursuit. Just like your left-hemisphere skills, such as mathematics or logic, your right-hemisphere skills can be improved and enhanced. If you score high on the next five tests, chances are you've steered your life into the more creative or visually oriented areas of endeavor.

8. Art Judgment Test

How many times have your heard (or said), "I may not know much about art, but I know what I like." Dr. Norman Meier, a University of Iowa psychologist, developed an interest in measuring aesthetic judgment, which served as the stimulus for a new abilities test. He wrote in the 1942 manual for the Art Judgment Test: "Aesthetic judgment is one of the most important, if not the most important, single factor in artistic competence. Without a fairly high degree of it, no artist produces meritorious work."

The Art Judgment Test grew out of research started in 1922, conducted by "one of the foremost research laboratories devoted to the investigation of specific talents." Meier's goal was to present 100 pairs of drawings, each one exploring a specific principle of aesthetic judgment. Your goal in taking the test is to evaluate the pair on the basis of that particular principle, selecting the alternative with the greater aesthetic value. Meier wrote that anyone with good aesthetic judgment should be able to sense the "perfect equilibrium of tension and volumes."

INSTRUCTIONS

The test that follows is an abbreviated version of the original Art Judgment Test. Beginning on the next page, you will be presented with 20 sets of drawings. The picture on the left will differ slightly from that on the right. You are to pick the variation that you find more aesthetically pleasing.

Below, for instance, are two versions of a medallion. The position of the child on the right is different in each version. You are to choose one as the better rendition. If you picked the picture on the left, you are answering correctly.

Before you begin, turn the page and tear out the Answer Sheet that you will use to record your responses. The differences between the pictures are described there as well. This test is untimed.

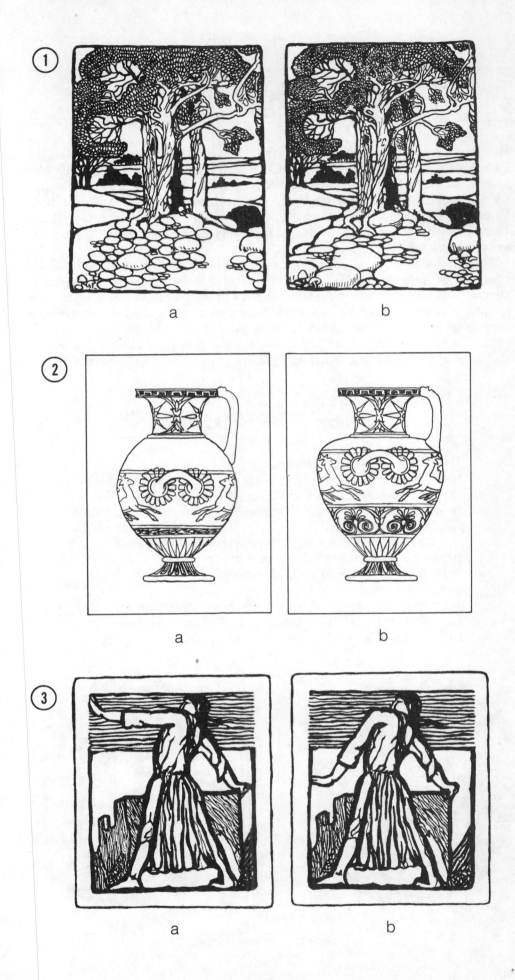

1   a   b

2   a   b

3   a   b

ANSWER SHEET

8. Art Judgment Test

A	B		DIFFERENCE
0	0	1.	foreground
0	0	2.	shape of vase
0	0	3.	position of left arm
0	0	4.	location of girls
0	0	5.	location of band
0	0	6.	arrangement of logs
0	0	7.	position of umbrella and girl's head
0	0	8.	foreground
0	0	9.	position of last (smallest) arch
0	0	10.	circular objects on table
0	0	11.	inclusion or omission of horns
0	0	12.	position of figures
0	0	13.	pattern of apron
0	0	14.	treatment of clouds
0	0	15.	background detail
0	0	16.	relative proportion of bridge and city
0	0	17.	background
0	0	18.	presence or absence of tower
0	0	19.	character of tracery work about animal
0	0	20.	location of horizon

(Tear Out)

ANSWER SHEET

8. Art Judgment Test

A	B		DIFFERENCE
O	O	1.	foreground
O	O	2.	shape of vase
O	O	3.	position of left arm
O	O	4.	location of girls
O	O	5.	location of band
O	O	6.	arrangement of logs
O	O	7.	position of umbrella and girl's head
O	O	8.	foreground
O	O	9.	position of last (smallest) arch
O	O	10.	circular objects on table
O	O	11.	inclusion or omission of horns
O	O	12.	position of figures
O	O	13.	pattern of apron
O	O	14.	treatment of clouds
O	O	15.	background detail
O	O	16.	relative proportion of bridge and city
O	O	17.	background
O	O	18.	presence or absence of tower
O	O	19.	character of tracery work about animal
O	O	20.	location of horizon

(Tear Out)

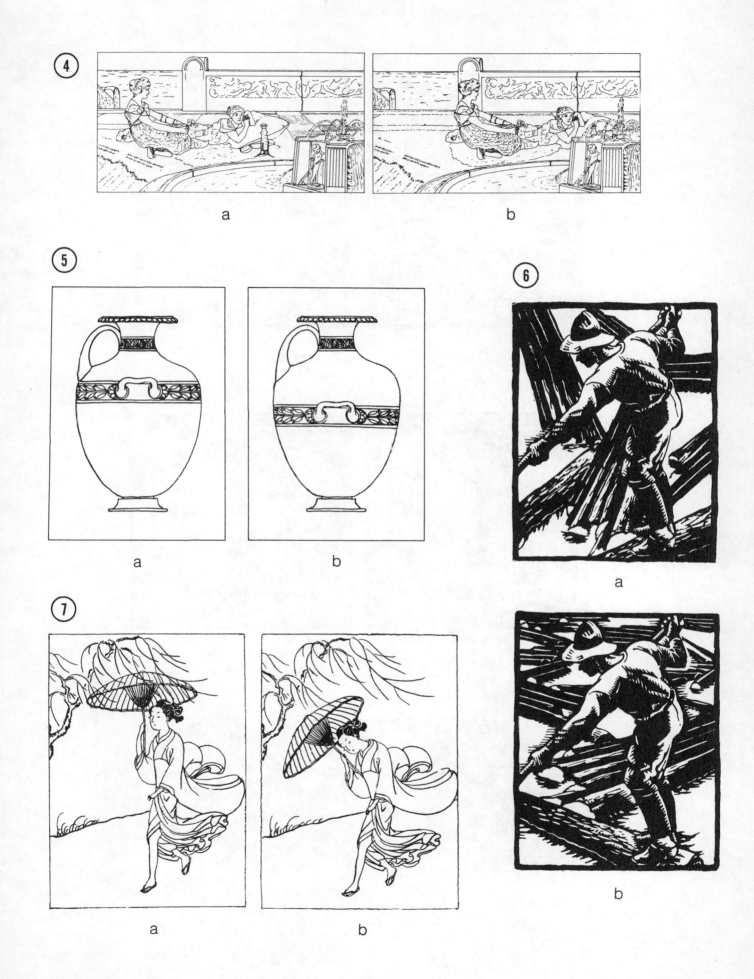

a

b

a

b

a

a

b

b

8

a   b

9

a   b

10

a   b

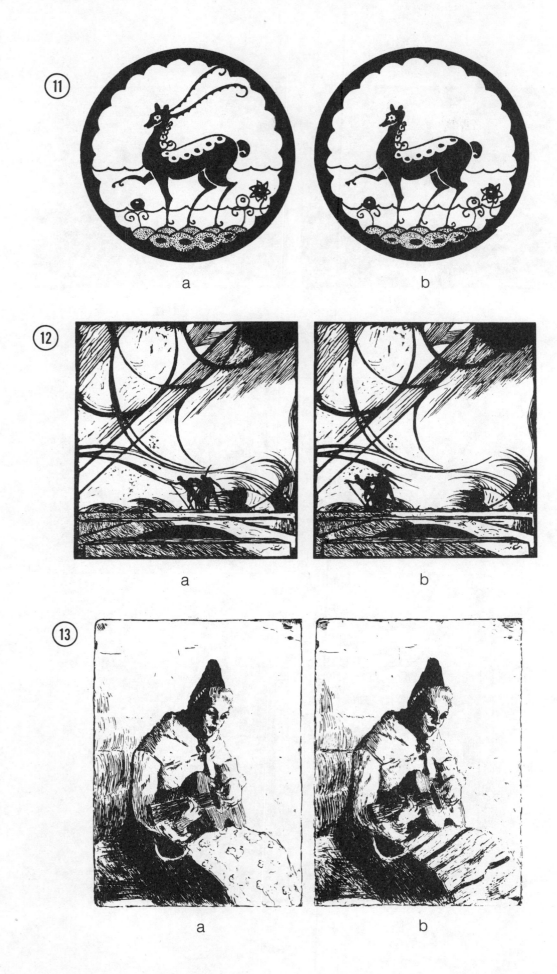

⑪

a

b

⑫

a

b

⑬

a

b

71

a   b

a   b

a   b

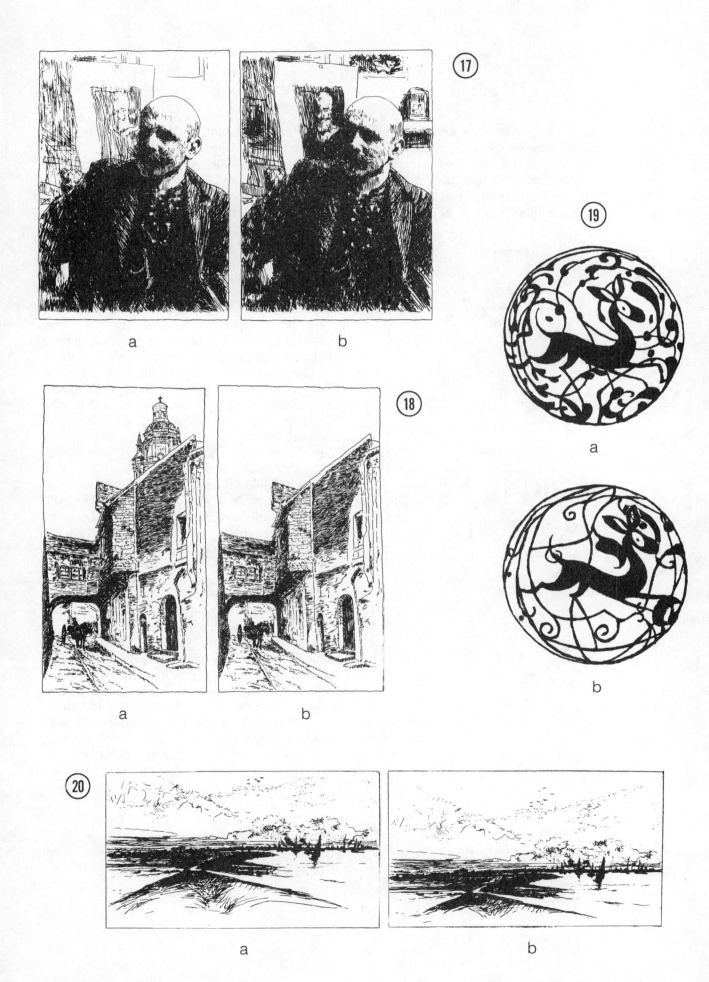

⑰

a   b

⑱

a   b

⑲

a

b

⑳

a   b

SCORING

To score the test, compare your answers on the Answer Sheet to those on the Scoring Key below. Give yourself 1 point for each correct answer, plus 1 extra point for each item marked with an asterisk (*) that you got right. Total possible: 26 points. Write your total score in the box below.

TOTAL
SCORE

SCORING KEY

1. b	*11. a
2. b	12. a
*3. a	*13. b
4. a	14. a
5. a	15. a
*6. b	*16. a
*7. b	17. a
8. b	18. a
9. b	19. a
10. a	20. b

INTERPRETATION

Ready to pick up your palette and hang your masterpieces in the Guggenheim? Dr. Meier would suggest some caution even if you scored well on the test (from 22 to 26). He would ask you to take your performance here and see if it is in harmony with other indicators of artistic ability, such as "high grades in art classes, craftsman ancestry, wide experience, and strong vitality."

At the very least, your high score indicates the ability to recognize the functions of rhythm, balance, and proportion, which are basic to all art. What you like in art probably does spring from a good, basic appreciation of quality and strong aesthetic judgment. That judgment is at least a start for such careers as interior design, clothing design, architecture, and, of course, art direction.

A score in the range of 17 to 21 indicates the level of aesthetic judgment found in most people. This means that you probably possess the overall ability to appreciate art and design, although you may get into friendly disagreements occasionally about why a painting belongs on a museum wall. It is very possible that in some specific artistic area, such as pottery or woodworking, you have developed your skills and judgment to a very high level, even though you're not highly sophisticated in others. Judgment in one area, however, if used as a base, can help you develop a good overall sense of aesthetic appreciation.

A low score on the Art Judgment Test (16 and below) suggests that you may not have had much exposure to art so far in your life. This may be related to your parents' lack of interest or to the limited requirements of the various jobs that you have had. You can, however, develop your aesthetic judgment through training and increased exposure to quality work. If you would like to increase your skills in this area, consider taking an art appreciation course through your local college or museum. You'll find that the skills you gain will add to your enjoyment of life far beyond selecting the better of two paintings.

9. Creative Associations Test

The creative individual is intelligent. But all intelligent people are not creative. Intelligence is known in psychological jargon as a "necessary but not sufficient" element of creativity. Research has shown other more specific attributes, such as originality, flexibility, and memory, to be important in the creative process. Assuming you have the necessary IQ base, you can proceed to evaluate the other abilities that are conducive to creativity.

One of the most successful attempts to develop a measure of a specific creative ability was made by psychologist Sarnoff Mednick in 1962. His test, the Remote Associates Test (RAT), was based on a definition of creativity as "the forming of associative elements into new combinations . . . . The more mutually remote the new combinations, the more creative the process or solution." Mednick's test involved presenting a word such as *chair* in a free-response format. The uncreative person, he felt, would respond with *table* and *sit*, but find further responding difficult. The creative person, on the other hand, would respond with *parliament, electric, swivel,* and continue responding, with a high percentage of the words only remotely associated with the original word.

Based on this view, Mednick developed the RAT to measure creativity. As he wrote, "Several words from mutually distant associative clusters must be presented to the subject; his task must be to provide mediating links between them." Research since Mednick's original work has established the concept of remote associations as a valid measure of one of the intriguing aspects of creativity. The following test is based on Mednick's views.

INSTRUCTIONS

In the Creative Association Test you will be presented with three words and asked to find a fourth word that is related to all three. For instance, what word do you think is related to these three words?

      paint   doll   cat   _____

The answer, in this case is house *— house* paint, doll*house, house* cat. *Here is another example:*

      stool   powder   ball   _____

If you were taking the test, you should have written the word foot *in the space provided —* foot*stool,* foot powder, foot*ball. As you can see, the fourth word may be related to the other three in various ways. Most people find this test very difficult. It is rarely completed by those who take it, so don't get discouraged.*

You have 20 minutes to complete this test, which begins on the next page. When your time is up, stop your work and turn the page to find your score.

1. call	pay	line	phone	1
2. end	burning	blue	hook	2
3. man	hot	sure	fire	3
4. stick	hair	ball	pin	4
5. blue	cake	cottage	cheese	5
6. man	wheel	high	chair	6
7. motion	poke	down	slow	7
8. stool	powder	ball	foot	8
9. line	birthday	surprise	party	9
10. wood	liquor	luck	hard	10
11. house	village	golf	green	11
12. plan	show	walker	floor	12
13. key	wall	precious	stone	13
14. bell	iron	tender	bar	14
15. water	pen	soda	fountain	15
16. base	snow	dance	ball	16
17. steady	kart	slow	go	17
18. up	book	charge	cover	18
19. tin	writer	my	type	19
20. leg	arm	person	chair	20
21. weight	pipe	pencil	lead	21
22. spin	tip	shape	top	22
23. sharp	thumb	tie	tack	23
24. out	band	night	stand	24
25. cool	house	fat	cat	25
26. back	short	light	stop	26
27. man	order	air	mail	27
28. bath	up	gum	bubble	28
29. ball	out	jack	black	29
30. up	deep	rear	end	30

SCORING KEY

1. phone
2. book
3. fire
4. pin
5. cheese
6. chair
7. slow
8. foot
9. party
10. hard
11. green
12. floor
13. stone
14. bar
15. fountain
16. ball
17. go
18. cover
19. type
20. chair
21. lead
22. top
23. tack
24. watch
25. cat
26. stop
27. mail
28. bubble
29. black
30. end

FOLD BACK TO SCORE

SCORING

To score this test, fold this page back on the dotted line and compare your answers to those on the Scoring Key. Give yourself 1 point for each correct answer.

TOTAL
SCORE

INTERPRETATION

The Creative Associations Test (CAT) requires that you go beyond the typical way in which you think of words. To do well on the CAT, you must have the ability to grasp mentally the common denominator of a group of words, and to do it under the pressure of a time limit. Your score on this test speaks to a broader concept than mere vocabulary; the test's words are simple and straightforward. The test requires, rather, a verbal flexibility that allows you to mentally arrange the words to find their common but remote thread.

Now to the scores themselves. A high score on the CAT is from 15 to 30 and indicates the ability to mix the skills that we've just discussed into an effective creative process. This type of ability is needed in almost any creative problem-solving situation where you must go beyond the factual data presented and develop an original solution. Dramatists, architects, speech writers, comedians, cartoonists, equipment troubleshooters, and advertising executives use such skills.

The middle range on CAT is from 8 to 14. A score here suggests the ability to think creatively but perhaps not in a timed situation. If that is the case for you, practice thinking creatively under self-imposed time pressure whenever possible. You'll probably find that your creative skills and your ability to work under a time limit will both improve.

A score in the range from 0 to 7 suggests difficulty with the kinds of skills needed to make creative associations, to work under time pressure, or both. If creativity is a quality that you see as valuable (and you probably do since you took this test), spend time analyzing your difficulties on this test and combine that information with the results from other tests in *The Brain Game*.

10. Purdue Creativity Test

by C. H. Lawshe and D.H. Harris

Question: When is a cup not a cup?

Answer: When it is used with string and becomes a walkie-talkie; or when it is used to prop a window open; or . . .

Measuring the creative process has fascinated and eluded researchers for many years. Most of what has been written about creativity could be called descriptive, speculative, or intended to stimulate research. The most promising research has focused on the specific skills and cognitive abilities that enable one to go beyond what has been termed *functional fixedness*, and see more uses for an object than the few most often attributed to it. To a functionally fixed person, the cup is primarily a drinking device or something that holds objects such as pencils. Going beyond those uses to others that are more remote is the hallmark of the creative individual.

Tapping this cognitive ability was the goal of Purdue psychologists C. H. Lawshe and Douglas Harris in 1957. Their purpose in creating the Purdue Creativity Test (PCT) was "to develop a test of creativity which would be suitable for use in the selection and placement of engineering personnel in industrial organizations." Today this type of test is used to measure creativity in children as well as adults and is administered for many different occupations.

INSTRUCTIONS

In the Purdue Creativity Test, you will be presented with eight objects similar to the example below. You are to list as many possible uses as you can for each object. Before beginning the test, study this example and note the different kinds of answers that may be appropriate.

1. roller on a treadmill
2. pack of Life Savers
3. section of heavy pipe
4. clay bead from necklace
5. rubber tube connector
6. vase
7. barrel of gun
8. part of barbershop pole

Give yourself 2 minutes for each object, 16 minutes in all. Take each item in order; do not skip ahead or go back to other items. Be sure to number each of your responses and keep them fairly brief. At the end of the 16 minutes, stop your work and turn the page to find your score.

①

_____
_____
_____
_____
_____
_____
_____
_____
_____

②

_____
_____
_____
_____
_____
_____
_____
_____
_____

③

_____
_____
_____
_____
_____
_____
_____
_____
_____

④

_____
_____
_____
_____
_____
_____
_____
_____
_____

⑤

⑥

⑦

⑧

SCORING

To find your score, go through your responses and eliminate any that are of such a general nature that they would apply to any item. Examples of these responses are *toy, ornament, thing, paperweight, test item, drawing.*

Next, for each item, eliminate any duplications in phrasing that express the same idea. An example of duplication is responding with *penny, nickel, dime, quarter,* and so on, when the central idea and an appropriate response would have been *coin.*

Finally, count the number of remaining responses, allowing 1 point for each one. Write your total score in the box below.

TOTAL
SCORE

TEST NORMS

PURDUE SCORING NORMS

TEST SCORE	PERCENTILE
54	99
44	95
41	90
36	80
33	70
30	60
28	50
25	40
22	30
19	20
16	10
12	5
10	1

INTERPRETATION

Creative people are often described as being able to visualize objects in space, to change their frame of reference easily, and to produce numerous problem-solving ideas. These characteristics imply abilities that are almost nonoverlapping with the linear skills attributed to the left hemisphere of the brain. The creative person can look at a situation and combine existing principles or mechanisms to produce new solutions to old problems. The noncreative person may then work out the details of the situation in a step-by-step manner.

The adjoining table gives you the scoring norms by Drs. Lawshe and Harris. Their norms were based on the performance of a large group of professional engineers working in industry. The percentiles in the right column indicate what percent of the norm group scored below the corresponding test score. If, for example, you got a 33 on the test, that would correspond to a percentile of 70, meaning that you scored higher than 70 percent of the norm group. Keep in mind as you compare your score to those in the chart that professional engineers may, because of their training, have a slight edge on you when it comes to generating multiple uses for a given object.

Scoring well on the Purdue Creativity Test may be its own best reward, since creative people are often described as relatively introverted — paying attention more to themselves than to social activities. High scores (32 and above) do suggest the ability to go beyond the functional fixedness discussed in the introduction to the test. Being able to think in a flexible manner is essential to jobs requiring creative problem-solving processes.

If you scored low (below 22) or at least lower than you would have liked, start your creative-skills training by thinking about how you can practice and improve these abilities. Look back over the test to see if your main problems were with the time pressure or a fixed style of thinking about the objects. Perhaps you could gain from one of the many mental puzzle books, finding them both helpful and fun. Even practicing a little each day by letting your mind play with alternate uses of everyday objects can help you develop your creative abilities.

11. Perceptual Motor Ability Test

by David R. Turner

How well can you think in three dimensions? When you see architectural plans for a home, can you visualize what that house would look like when built? Did you do well in the solid geometry part of your math courses?

These are just three of the questions that your performance on the next test will answer. The Perceptual Motor Ability Test (PMAT) measures your ability to imagine the surfaces and design of an object before it is constructed by asking you to visualize it based on flat, two-dimensional drawings. To do well you will need to mentally manipulate the designs presented, folding them in your mind.

The skill tested by the PMAT has long been considered an important intellectual ability. Major tests of specific abilities, such as the frequently administered Differential Aptitude Test, include a large number of similar items as part of the test battery. The PMAT is a challenging way for you to tap one of the intellectual skills of the right hemisphere of the brain.

INSTRUCTIONS

In the Perceptual Motor Ability Test, you will be presented with 14 sets of drawings. Each one shows a cardboard box, followed by four drawings of the way it might look if it were unfolded. You are to choose the cardboard pattern that could be unfolded from the numbered box and write your response in the space provided.

Give yourself five minutes to complete this test. When your time is up, stop your work and turn the page to find your score.

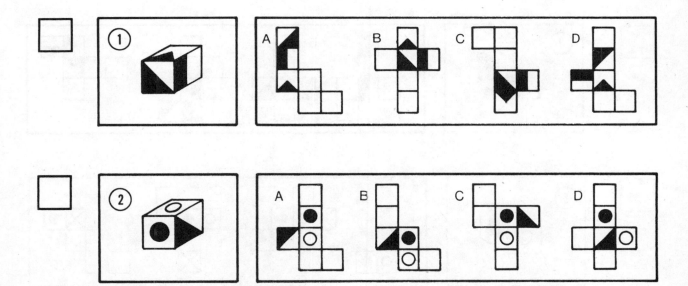

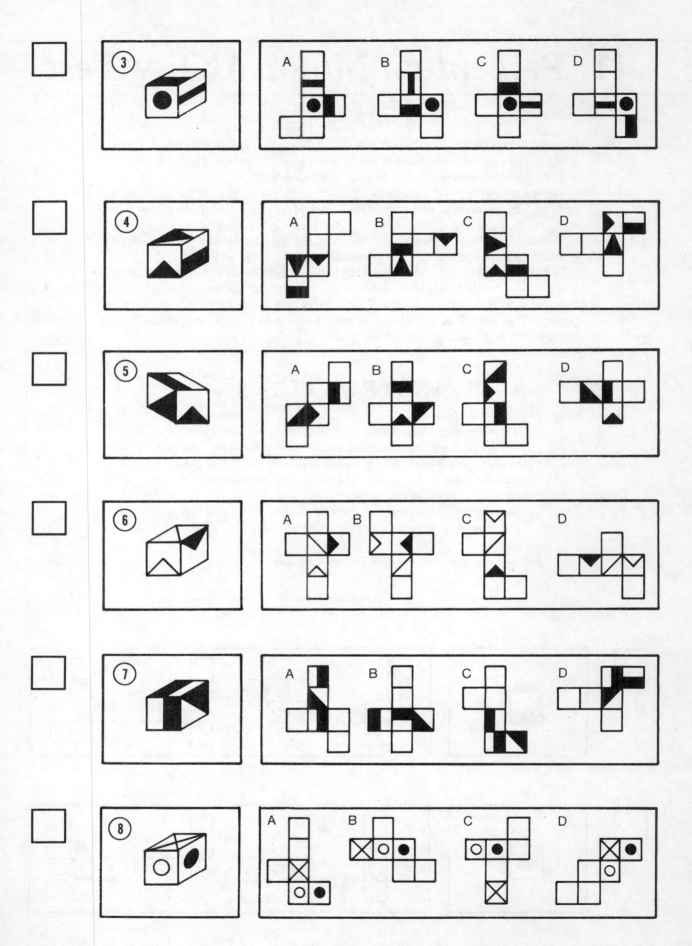

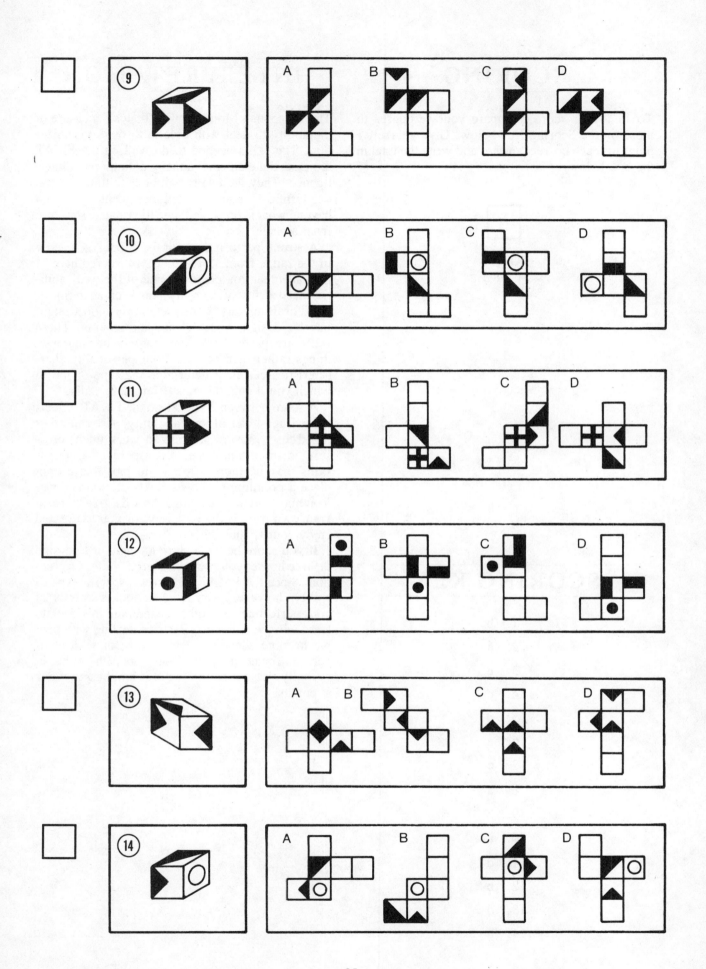

85

SCORING

To find your score, compare your responses to those on the Scoring Key below. Give yourself 1 point for each correct answer and write the total in the box below.

**TOTAL
SCORE**

SCORING KEY

1. b
2. a
3. c
4. c
5. d
6. a
7. c
8. a
9. b
10. a
11. d
12. b
13. d
14. b

INTERPRETATION

The Perceptual Motor Ability Test is a measure of the ability to deal with objects through visualization. The skills needed to do well on the PMAT are essential elements in many definitions of intelligence. They include the abilities to think in spatial terms, to manipulate things mentally, to go beyond what is presented, and to visualize structure from a plan.

A strong performance on the PMAT is a score in the range from 12 to 14. If you scored here, it indicates that you possess some of the basic abilities needed for success in fields such as architecture, drafting, art, construction, fashion design, interior design, and tool and die making. These skills are particularly important in dealing with things rather than people. Your personality characteristics can help determine the type of job in which you'll gain the most from these skills.

A score between 8 and 11 on the PMAT reflects an average level of spatial ability. As with other timed tests, how well you can work under pressure is important here. Your perceptual motor skills may be more effective in jobs that do not place a premium on how quickly the job is done. You may find that designing the kids' tree house at your own pace is the best way for you to use and enjoy your spatial skills.

If you score below 8, hire a neighbor to design the tree house; you can take charge of the construction. Since the PMAT measures a specific type of ability, however, you need to look carefully at your performance in other chapters in this book to learn what you do best. Perhaps dealing with people in more socially oriented jobs, or with numbers in financial occupations, or with words in verbally based fields would emphasize your strengths.

12. Perspective Analysis Test

by Alfred S. Lewerenz

Psychology and art combine to convince us that a two-dimensional surface can represent three-dimensional space. In both disciplines the term for this illusion is *perspective*. Perspective skills in art date back to the ancient Greeks, but were not emphasized until the 14th and 15th centuries, when there was great interest in optics and mathematical laws. The *Last Supper* by Leonardo da Vinci, painted during that period, is still considered a perfectly realized representation of the various perspective techniques.

The ability to analyze critically the composition of a painting is an essential skill for anyone involved with art. An examination of art courses and programs shows that anyone interested in pursuing art as a career must have skills in using and evaluating perspective. In 1927, Dr. Alfred S. Lewerenz developed a series of tests to measure fundamental artistic abilities. Dr. Lewerenz analyzed the content of visual art courses to determine which skills and abilities were essential to success in art. Three of his nine tests deal with perspective, a knowledge of which he saw as central to overall artistic ability. We present those three tests to you just as Dr. Lewerenz administered them as part of his art test battery over 50 years ago.

INSTRUCTIONS

In the Perspective Analysis Test you will be presented with 16 line drawings. Each of the drawings will have one or more problems with perspective. You are to mark the incorrect line or lines with an X. For instance, in the example below, the drawing of the cube has a line at the wrong angle to achieve perspective. This line has been marked correctly with an X.

Give yourself 15 minutes to complete this test. When your time is up, stop your work and turn the page to find your score.

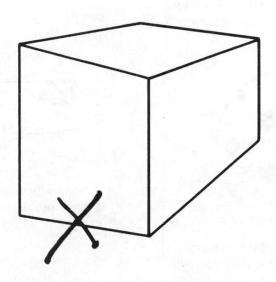

1. Mark with an X the line that is wrong in this drawing of a tin can.

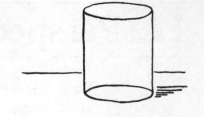

2. Mark with an X the edge of the flower pot that is incorrectly drawn.

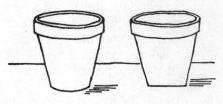

3. Mark with an X the edge of the cylinder that is incorrectly drawn.

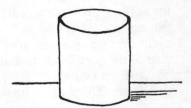

4. Mark with an X the object that is incorrectly drawn.

5. Mark with an X each of the three round spots on the cube that are incorrectly drawn.

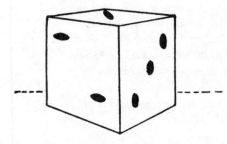

6. Mark with an X each of the three round spots on the child's ball that are incorrectly drawn.

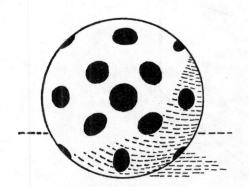

7. Mark with an X each of the two lines around the lighthouse that are incorrectly drawn.

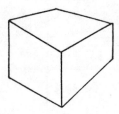

8. Mark with an X the edge of the box that is incorrectly drawn.

9. Mark with an X each of the three incorrectly drawn surfaces.

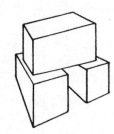

10. Mark with an X the edge of the book that is incorrectly drawn.

11. Mark with an X five incorrectly drawn parts of this building.

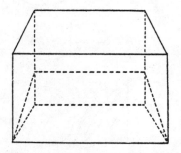

14. Mark with an X the horizontal line that is incorrectly drawn in this transparent box.

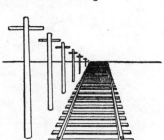

12. Mark with an X the rail of the railroad track that is incorrectly drawn.

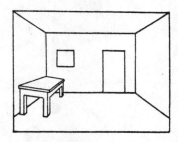

15. Mark with an X any two untrue or incorrect lines in this drawing.

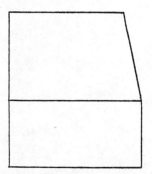

13. Mark with an X the edge of the box that is incorrectly drawn. The center of the box is straight in front of you.

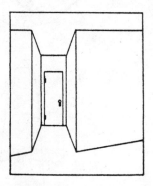

16. Mark with an X each of the two untrue or incorrect lines in this hall with connecting passage.

SCORING KEY

1. 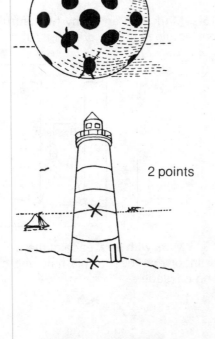 1 point

2. 1 point

3. 1 point

4. 1 point

5. 3 points

6. 3 points

7. 2 points

SCORING

To score the test, compare your answers with those on the Scoring Key. For each one of your X's that matches an X on the Key, give yourself 1 point. Note that some pictures have several possible points.

Now it is necessary to divide your score into three parts. Write your total scores for items 1 through 7, 8 through 11, and 12 through 16 in the boxes below.

ITEMS 1-7 ITEMS 8-11 ITEMS 12-16

☐ ☐ ☐

PART I PART II PART III

8. 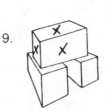 1 point

9. 3 points

10. 1 point

11. Allowed as 1 of 5

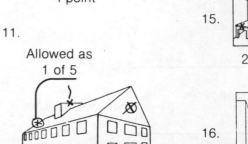 5 points

12. 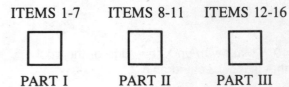 1 point

13. 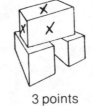 1 point

14. 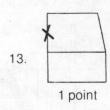 1 point

15. 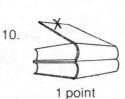 2 points

16. 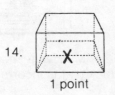 2 points

90

INTERPRETATION

To interpret your performance on the Perspective Analysis Test, follow the steps listed below.
1. Circle the three scores in the table below that equal your scores in the three parts of the test.
2. Take the corresponding ratings from the right-hand column and enter them into the appropriate boxes below your scores.
3. Add your three ratings and place that number in the Total of Ratings box.
4. Divide that ratings total by 3 to get your Ratings Average and enter that in the appropriate box.
5. Circle your Ratings Average in the table labeled Perspective Analysis Norms and find your ability rating.

PART I	PART II	PART III	DESCRIPTION	RATING
(Items 1–7)	(Items 8–11)	(Items 12–16)		
12	9, 10	7	very strong	1
10, 11	6–8	5, 6	strong	2
9	4, 5	3, 4	average	3
6–8	1–3	2	weak	4
0–5	0	0, 1	very weak	5

☐ + ☐ + ☐

☐ divided by 3 = ☐

TOTAL OF RATINGS   RATINGS AVERAGE

Although Dr. Lewerenz saw overall intelligence as an element in perspective analysis ability. he viewed experience and specific training as having the most crucial impact on the development of such skills. A strong ability in perspective analysis is related, in Dr. Lewerenz's view, to a certain type of mind-set. It "may be likened to a scientific attitude toward pictorial representation."

Scoring well on the PAT indicates an ability to critically observe your surroundings, much like the way in which a scientist analyzes a large body of data. Skill in this area can be very important in fields that require such exact observation — for example, geology, surgery, engineering, art, and meteorology.

If you did not score as well as you would have liked, take heart from Dr. Lewerenz's view that this skill is heavily influenced by training. Given an interest in increasing your skills in this area (and given a certain level of basic intelligence), you can profit from specific training in using and analyzing perspective. Such training is also likely to improve your overall observational skills and increase what you can learn from the world around you.

TEST NORMS

PERSPECTIVE ANALYSIS NORMS

RATINGS AVERAGE	ABILITY RATINGS
1.0–2.3	very strong
2.4–2.8	strong
2.9–3.2	average
3.3–3.6	weak
3.7–5.0	very weak

The Letter
by Pierre Bonnard
The National Gallery of Art
Washington, D.C.

CHAPTER THREE

THE SOFTWARE

of a culture — law, art, music, science, and technology — are the result of a collaborative effort by both the left and right hemispheres of the brain. While the left hemisphere manifests a clear advantage in dealing with language and speech, understanding the subtle meaning of the words requires processing in the right hemisphere. And, although recognizing forms and spatial relationships may be a right-brain function, drawing an accurate picture of something does require both hemispheres — the right for the overall contour and the left for the details and the internal elements.

This collaboration between the brain's hemispheres can be compared to the programming or software of a computer. In order for a computer (the hardware) to operate intelligently and effectively it must have a software program that tells it how to creatively utilize its own system. In the same way, our brains, with their specific neurophysiological functions, must have an overall intelligence — or mind — that directs the various components to do the proper thing at the proper time. Using the software of our minds is necessary to express newly generated ideas.

While the left hemisphere is the verbalizer and the right is the visualizer, the most important intellectual achievements seem to come from whole-brain processes, where both hemispheres are engaged in generating and transmitting information. Scientific research, for example, may appear to be a logical, linear, and thoroughly left-brain approach to dealing with information. In fact, what the scientists do not reveal in their findings are the wonderings, dreams, and hunches that steered their research toward original solutions. The creative, intuitive, right-hemisphere approach is actually the basis of the most significant accomplishments in such left-hemisphere disciplines as physics, mathematics, and linguistics. And conversely, our left-brain skills help us fit intuitive, conceptual hypotheses into verbal or numerical modes so that they can be explicitly explained and understood. To convey an idea, or to transmit it in a functional form, it must be clothed in comprehensible words and images for external use.

The tests that follow will measure what we call your software abilities, the power of analyzing the presented information or ideas and expressing them in an effective fashion. Some of the tests will measure how well you can understand the subtle meanings of words and the extent of your ability to express yourself accurately. Other tests will look at your ability to visualize and then analyze given information. If you do well on the next seven tests, you will be demonstrating a combined intellectual strength in both hemispheres of the brain.

13. Analytical Abilities Test

The Analytical Abilities Test explores the theory of the logical syllogism. A syllogism consists of three statements; the first two lead to the third, which is the conclusion. As an argument in logic, the syllogism was first proposed by Aristotle. According to Aristotelian logic, all reasoning can be put into syllogistic form and then evaluated for its validity. This idea has been basic to the development of Western thought.

Aristotle's theory deals primarily with the concept of classes or categories. For example, some of A is B; all of B is C; therefore, some of A is C. Such a syllogism can be illustrated by a Venn diagram, a series of circles used to graphically describe the logical process.

The first part of this test involves diagrams, and tests your ability to apply logical principles to problems in which one class may contain or be contained within another.

The second part of the test involves a somewhat different type of logical process. You are asked here to develop your own method of systematically diagramming a sequence of things or events. The next step requires you to deduce new information from that ordering and come up with the correct answer.

INSTRUCTIONS

To take the Analytical Abilities Test, turn the page and tear out the Answer Sheet that you will use to record your responses. Because the test deals with logical arrangements and relationships, you may find it helpful to make diagrams of the situations described in the space provided.

For example, suppose you are told:
 (a) Judy is a year older than Kate.
 (b) Kate is two years older than Joyce.
 (c) Joyce is a year younger than Pat.

A horizontal line could represent a year's difference, with older individuals above the younger. Thus you could construct the following diagram:

(a)	(b)	(c)
Judy		
Kate	Kate	
		Pat
	Joyce	Joyce

Putting the three sections together you could arrive at the following order:

Judy
Kate
Pat
Joyce

This final diagram enables you to answer questions about chronological order and the age relationship between any two parties.

There are 30 items in the test and you have 30 minutes in which to complete them. When your time is up, stop your work and turn the page to find your score.

© 1980 Arco Publishing, Inc. From The Graduate Record Examination Aptitude Test by the Arco Editorial Board.

In questions 1 through 15, you are to choose from five diagrams the one that illustrates the relationship among three given classes better than any other diagram offered.

There are three possible relationships between any two different classes:

indicates that one class is completely contained in the other but not vice versa.

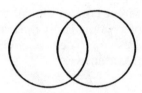

indicates that neither class is completely contained in the other, but the two do have members in common.

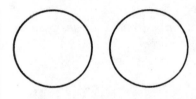

indicates that there are no members in common.

Note: The sizes of the circles do not indicate relative sizes of classes.

Questions 1 through 8 are based on the following diagrams:

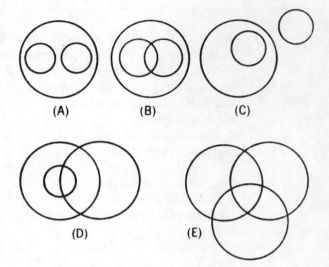

1. locusts, mosquitoes, insects

2. commanding officers, agreements, treaties

3. rubies, diamonds, precious stones

4 midgets, short people, toddlers

5. professional athletes, amateur scientists, college graduates

6. cousins, males, relatives

7. liquids, chicken soup, rainwater

8. portrait painters, artists, landscape painters

ANSWER SHEET

13. Analytical Abilities Test

	a	b	c	d	e			a	b	c	d	e
1.	0	0	0	0	0		16.	0	0	0	0	0
2.	0	0	0	0	0		17.	0	0	0	0	0
3.	0	0	0	0	0		18.	0	0	0	0	0
4.	0	0	0	0	0		19.	0	0	0	0	0
5.	0	0	0	0	0		20.	0	0	0	0	0
6.	0	0	0	0	0		21.	0	0	0	0	0
7.	0	0	0	0	0		22.	0	0	0	0	0
8.	0	0	0	0	0		23.	0	0	0	0	0
9.	0	0	0	0	0		24.	0	0	0	0	0
10.	0	0	0	0	0		25.	0	0	0	0	0
11.	0	0	0	0	0		26.	0	0	0	0	0
12.	0	0	0	0	0		27.	0	0	0	0	0
13.	0	0	0	0	0		28.	0	0	0	0	0
14.	0	0	0	0	0		29.	0	0	0	0	0
15.	0	0	0	0	0		30.	0	0	0	0	0

NOTES

(Tear Out)

ANSWER SHEET

13. Analytical Abilities Test

	a	b	c	d	e			a	b	c	d	e
1.	O	O	O	O	O		16.	O	O	O	O	O
2.	O	O	O	O	O		17.	O	O	O	O	O
3.	O	O	O	O	O		18.	O	O	O	O	O
4.	O	O	O	O	O		19.	O	O	O	O	O
5.	O	O	O	O	O		20.	O	O	O	O	O
6.	O	O	O	O	O		21.	O	O	O	O	O
7.	O	O	O	O	O		22.	O	O	O	O	O
8.	O	O	O	O	O		23.	O	O	O	O	O
9.	O	O	O	O	O		24.	O	O	O	O	O
10.	O	O	O	O	O		25.	O	O	O	O	O
11.	O	O	O	O	O		26.	O	O	O	O	O
12.	O	O	O	O	O		27.	O	O	O	O	O
13.	O	O	O	O	O		28.	O	O	O	O	O
14.	O	O	O	O	O		29.	O	O	O	O	O
15.	O	O	O	O	O		30.	O	O	O	O	O

NOTES

(Tear Out)

Questions 9 through 15 are based on the following diagrams:

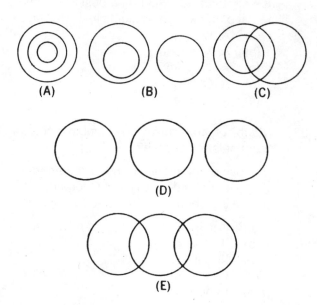

9. navigators, aircrewmen, war veterans

10. aunts, women, lovers of children

11. seconds, days, years

12. grave robbers, MD's, medical students

13. sketch pads, people who draw, cartoonists

14. food, milk products, cheese

15. competitive divers, diving boards, athletes

Each question or set of questions below is based on a reading passage or collection of numbered statements. In some cases it may be helpful to draw a diagram. Choose the best answer for each question.

SET I

In putting together a school newspaper, four editors are needed: the managing editor, the news editor, the sports editor, and the entertainment editor.

The managing editor can schedule work only Wednesday mornings, Thursday afternoons, and all day Friday.

The news editor can schedule work only on Monday mornings, and all day Tuesday and Thursday.

The sports editor can schedule work only Monday afternoons, Tuesday mornings, and all day Wednesday.

The entertainment editor can schedule work all day Monday and Wednesday only.

16. If the managing editor cannot start until each of the others has completed at least a full day of work, when is the earliest the managing editor can work?
    (a) Monday afternoon
    (b) Tuesday afternoon
    (c) Wednesday morning
    (d) Thursday afternoon
    (e) Friday morning

17. One of the editors must work completely alone for a whole day in order to prevent confusion and disorder. If no other editor can afford to lose his or her available time, then the only possible editor privileged with working alone is
    (a) the entertainment editor on Monday
    (b) the news editor on Tuesday
    (c) the sports editor on Wednesday
    (d) the news editor on Thursday
    (e) the managing editor on Friday

SET II

In the United States, most marriages between two people under 21 years of age end in divorce. More children are being raised by one parent. Therefore, the practice of marrying young should be abandoned.

18. The argument is based on the assumption(s) that:
    I. The fact that more children are being raised by one parent is linked to the failure of so many young marriages.
    II. It is undesirable to have a child raised by a single parent.
    III. Marriage between people over 21 years of age is better than marriage between people under 21.

    (a) I only
    (b) II only
    (c) II and III only
    (d) I and II only
    (e) I, II, and III

19. The argument would be weakened if it were noted that:
    (a) A broken home can be detrimental to a child in his or her early years.
    (b) Most parents who are raising a child alone were married when older than 21 years of age.
    (c) There are marriages between people over 21 that end in divorce.
    (d) Child custody is more often than before awarded to the father.
    (e) Most people who marry young do not have a long engagement.

20. The argument would be strengthened if it were noted that:
    (a) Most young marriages take place without the knowledge of the parents.
    (b) Most parents raising a child alone were wed when over 21 years of age.
    (c) Children under the care of one young parent have been consistently found to have emotional problems.
    (d) There are children who, because they were raised by only one parent, are more independent.
    (e) In Europe, marriages are determined by the family when the bride and groom are barely adolescents.

SET III

Marion Keene, a scientist, is trying to find a cure for the common cold using four ingredients. She can choose from the stable chemicals A, B, and C and the unstable chemicals W, X, Y, and Z. In order for the formula not to explode, there must be two stable chemicals in it. Also, certain chemicals cannot be mixed because of their reaction together.

Chemical B cannot be mixed with chemical W.
Chemical C cannot be mixed with chemical Y.
Chemical Y cannot be mixed with chemical Z.

21. If Ms. Keene calculated that Y is the most important chemical and must be used in the formula, which other ingredients must be part of the cure?
    (a) A, B, and W
    (b) A, B, and X
    (c) A, B, and Z
    (d) A, C, and X
    (e) B, C, and X

22. If Ms. Keene rejected chemical B because of its possible side effects but decided to use chemical Z, which is a possible combination of the four ingredients in the formula?
    (a) A, W, X, and Z
    (b) A, X, Y, and Z
    (c) A, W, Y, and Z
    (d) A, C, W, and Z
    (e) A, C, Y, and Z

23. Which of the following combinations of chemicals is possible?
    I. using chemicals Y and W together
    II. using chemicals B and C together
    III. using chemicals W, X, and Z together

    (a) I only
    (b) II only
    (c) III only
    (d) I and II only
    (e) I and III only

24. Which of the following can never be true?
    I. If chemical C is used, chemical Z is added.
    II. If chemical B is not used, chemical Y is added.
    III. If chemical C is used, chemical W is added.

    (a) I, II, and III
    (b) II only
    (c) III only
    (d) I and II only
    (e) II and III only

25. Which of the following must always be true?
    I. If chemical C is used, chemical W must be added.
    II. If chemical Y is used, chemical B must be added.
    III. If chemical C is not used, chemical W cannot be added.

    (a) I and II only
    (b) I and III only
    (c) II and III only
    (d) II only
    (e) I, II, and III

SET IV

A research team did a study in which they starved monkeys for three days and then tested their intelligence by letting them run a maze that they had run before the three-day fast. Results showed that monkeys' maze-running times had slowed, thus supporting the view that the lower intelligence of people in poor countries is the result of malnutrition.

26. Which of the following assumptions are made in the argument?

   I. The effects of malnutrition on monkey intelligence are parallel to those on human intelligence.
   II. The proper food has a direct correlation to the intelligence level in monkeys and people.
   III. Captive monkeys are reasonably more intelligent than wild monkeys.

   (a) I only
   (b) II only
   (c) III only
   (d) I and II only
   (e) II and III only

27. Which of the following statements would weaken the argument?
   (a) Monkeys in the wild are often unable to maintain a proper diet from the resources around them.
   (b) Monkeys are prone to short memories.
   (c) The intelligence level of high school students in the United States varies from state to state.
   (d) Tests of intelligence are becoming more and more accurate.
   (e) Many people in poor nations have never received intelligence tests.

28. Which of the following statements would strengthen the argument?
   (a) Monkeys are used to going for short periods of time without food.
   (b) Some sections of the United States, a wealthy country, have undernourished people living within them.
   (c) Countries which have increased their food production have also increased the level of intelligence among their people.
   (d) Poor countries also have a health problem due to the improper diets of their people.
   (e) In poor countries, the educational facilities are usually limited.

SET V

A coin collector owns five vintage South American coins, each having a different value.
   (1) Coin D is worth twice as much as coin E.
   (2) Coin E is worth four and one half times as much as coin F.
   (3) Coin F is worth half as much as coin G.
   (4) Coin G is worth half as much as coin H.
   (5) Coin H is worth less than coin D, but more than coin F.

29. Which of the following represents the relative order of the coins from the highest to lowest value?
   (a) D, E, G, H, and F
   (b) E, G, H, D, and F
   (c) H, F, G, D, and E
   (d) F, D, G, E, and H
   (e) D, E, H, G, and F

30. Which of the numbered statements above is not necessary to determine the correct order of the coins?
   (a) statement 1
   (b) statement 4
   (c) statement 3
   (d) statement 2
   (e) statement 5

SCORING

To score the test, compare your responses on the Answer Sheet to those on the Scoring Key. Give yourself 1 point for each correct answer and write the total in the box below. For a complete discussion of the answers, read the Explanatory Answers section.

TOTAL
SCORE

SCORING KEY

1.	a	16.	c
2.	c	17.	e
3.	a	18.	d
4.	b	19.	b
5.	e	20.	c
6.	d	21.	b
7.	a	22.	d
8.	b	23.	e
9.	c	24.	b
10.	c	25.	c
11.	d	26.	d
12.	e	27.	b
13.	b	28.	c
14.	a	29.	e
15.	b	30.	e

INTERPRETATION

A high score on the two parts of the Analytical Abilities Test is from 22 to 30 points, average is from 11 to 21, and a low score is from 0 to 10. A strong performance shows a high level of linear problem-solving skill combined with an ability to view things in their totality. In the diagram section you were required to determine how objects and various categories of objects were interrelated. You could have attacked these problems using a trial and error process, placing the objects into each possible Venn diagram. Such a rigid linear process is slow, however, and not likely to produce a high score under timed conditions. If you did well, you most likely attempted to grasp the concepts in a holistic manner, determining the relationships of the classes and then matching that answer to the appropriate diagram.

Scoring well on the second section of the test requires an ability to systematically diagram the relationships given in the problem. This is an intellectual process that we frequently call upon in our daily activities. We are often presented with a sequence or ordering of things or events and asked to make a decision based on that information. Doing well in such situations requires you to grasp and integrate all of the presented factors. Then more linear, deductive logic takes over as you perceive the correct response or relationship. This test takes that one step further and requires you to make such determinations quickly.

The Instructions suggested that you draw a diagram of the presented information. If you did not do well on this section — at least not as well as you would have liked — think about the process that you first used to integrate the data. Did you try to answer without a diagram? Was your major difficulty in conceiving of the diagram itself? That first integrative step is an all-important one.

Think about the biologist seeking to understand a partially hidden process, or the repairman troubleshooting an unusual equipment breakdown. Each must first integrate various bits of information in order to logically deduce the next step. The police detective and the system analyst also find this ability essential. And while certain occupations rely especially heavily on such logical processes, many daily decisions demand these skills as well. If you scored well on the test, those decision situations are probably an enjoyable challenge for you. If you did not score well overall, remember that you can improve your logical skills with practice.

EXPLANATORY ANSWERS

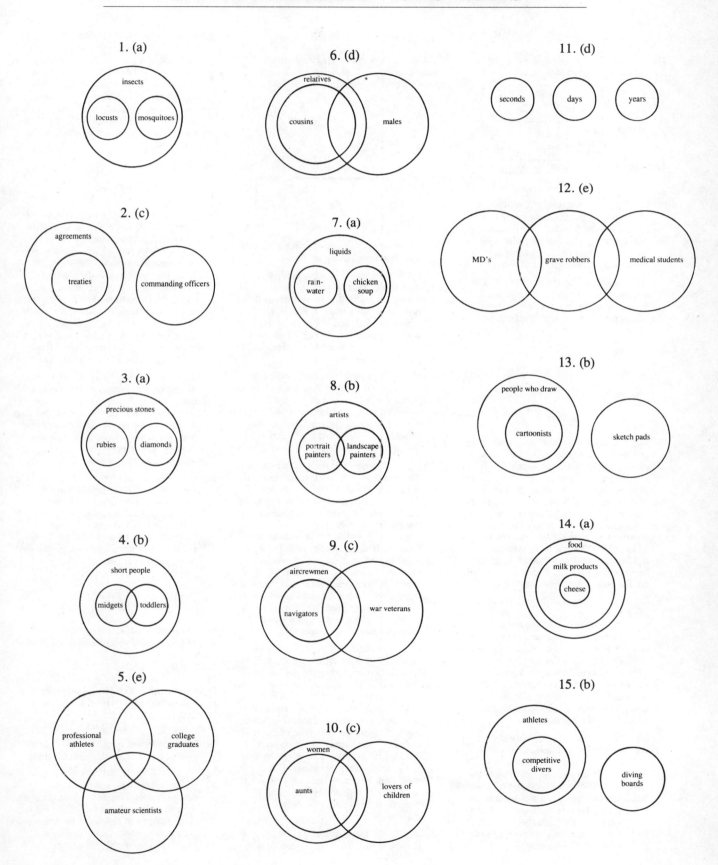

1. (a)
insects
locusts mosquitoes

2. (c)
agreements
treaties
commanding officers

3. (a)
precious stones
rubies diamonds

4. (b)
short people
midgets toddlers

5. (e)
professional athletes
college graduates
amateur scientists

6. (d)
relatives
cousins males

7. (a)
liquids
rain-water chicken soup

8. (b)
artists
portrait painters landscape painters

9. (c)
aircrewmen
navigators war veterans

10. (c)
women
aunts lovers of children

11. (d)
seconds days years

12. (e)
MD's grave robbers medical students

13. (b)
people who draw
cartoonists
sketch pads

14. (a)
food
milk products
cheese

15. (b)
athletes
competitive divers
diving boards

EXPLANATORY ANSWERS

SET I

The schedules of the four editors can be represented by the following chart:

	M	T	W	Th	F
Managing editor			✕		✕ ✕ ✕
News editor	✕		✕ ✕		✕ ✕
Sports editor		✕ ✕		✕ ✕	
Entertainment editor	✕ ✕			✕ ✕	

16. (c). It can be seen that by Tuesday afternoon, all but the managing editor have worked a full day. The managing editor cannot work Tuesday afternoon, but the next best time scheduled is Wednesday morning.

17. (e). Looking at the above diagram, it is obvious that only on Friday can the managing editor work all day without infringing on the others' available time.

SET II

18. (d). The argument states that, since many children are being raised by only one parent, young marriages should be avoided, thus assuming a link between the two. Because the argument cites the cases of children being raised by one parent as a point in favor of abolishing young marriages, it can be deduced that the argument assumes this situation to be undesirable. The argument assumes nothing about the outcome of marriages between older adults. Therefore, I and II are the only assumptions made.

19. (b). If a broken home is detrimental to a child's development, the argument to avoid divorce among young couples is strengthened. The argument opposes young marriages which ultimately cause children to be raised by one parent. Choice (b) would make the argument worthless. Marriages of those over 21, and the decision of child custody, and the length of engagement have nothing to do with the point of contention.

20. (c). Choices (a) and (e) neither strengthen nor weaken the argument. Choices (b) and (d) weaken the case. Choice (b) claims that marriages of those over 21 are linked to single parenthood and (d) states that some children are actually better off because they have been raised by only one parent. Choice (c) is therefore the best since it deals with the problems of children without two parents.

SET III

A diagram such as the following can be made to clarify the relationships among the different chemicals:

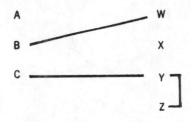

A line connecting two chemicals indicates that they are mutually exclusive.

21. (b). If chemical Y is being used, then chemical C must be rejected, and chemicals A and B must be used as the two stable ingredients. If B is used, W cannot be used, and Y cannot be used with Z. Therefore, the only chemical left is X. Thus, if Y is used, chemicals A, B, and X must also be used.

22. (d). If chemical Z is used, chemical Y cannot be used. Since B is rejected, both A and C must be used as the stable ingredients. Both chemicals X and W are left and either can be used, but, of the combinations listed, A, C, X, and Z is not included where A, C, W, and Z is.

23. (e). If chemical Y is used, C cannot be. Therefore, both A and B must be added. Since B is added, W cannot be used. Therefore, chemicals Y and W cannot be used together. If both B and C are used, this eliminates only A, W, and Y. Chemicals Z and X can be used in the formula. If all three chemicals W, X, and Z are used then there can be only one more ingredient added. Neither W, X, nor Z are stable chemicals, and thus it is impossible to have the required two stable ingredients in the formula. Therefore, W, X, and Z cannot be used all together. Choices I and III are impossible.

24. (b). If chemical C is used, Y cannot be added. Since Y is not an ingredient in the formula, Z may or may not be used. Thus, the combination of chemicals C and Z is not impossible. If chemical B is not used, then A and C must be used as the two stable ingredients. Since C is being used, Y cannot be used. Therefore, if B is not used, then neither can Y be used. If C is added, then either A or B can be used as the other stable ingredient. If B is used, then W cannot be used; but if A is used, it is all right to use chemical W. Therefore, choice II is the only impossible combination.

25. (c). If chemical C is used, either A or B may be used. If A is used, then W may

be added. But if B is added, W must be rejected. Therefore, chemicals C and W need not be used together. If Y is used, C cannot be added. Therefore, A and B must be added as the two stable ingredients. If chemical C is not used, then A and B must be used; but W cannot be used with B. Therefore, II and III are the only choices which must always be true.

SET IV

26. (d). The argument draws its conclusion from the study done with monkeys and thus assumes that factors affecting monkey intelligence have a parallel effect on human intelligence. The argument states that ignorance is the result of improper diet. Therefore, it must assume a correlation between the two. The study makes no reference to (and therefore no assumption about) the difference in intelligence between captive and wild monkeys. Therefore, only I and II are assumptions made by the argument.

27. (b). Even if monkeys are prone to short memories, this cannot be the reason for their inability to run the maze as quickly as on their initial run. The statement does suggest, however, that lack of food may have had nothing to do with their slower running time. Choice (b), therefore, would weaken the argument.

28. (c). Only choice (c) would help strengthen the argument. If the problem of malnutrition were conquered, then, according to the argument, the spread of ignorance should be narrowed. An increase in the level of intelligence as a result of the increase of food production is a good supportive fact.

SET V

To answer these questions, one must determine the relationships among the given statements:
From statement 1: $D = 2E$
From statement 2: $E = 4.5F$ or $2E = 9F$
From statement 3: $G = 2F$ or $4.5G = 9F$
From statement 4: $2G = H$ or $4.5G = 2.25H$
From statement 5: $D > H > F$
Therefore: $D = 2E = 2.25H = 4.5G = 9F$

29. (e). We can see from the above that the correct order, from the highest value to the lowest is: D, E, H, G, and F.

30. (e). In answering question 29, we determined the correct order of the coins without using statement 5. There are no other statements which can be eliminated. Statements 1–14 are all specifically related to one another by a letter.

14. Opposites Test

by Andrew Tenant Wylie

Antonyms — that is, words that are opposite in meaning — have a significant place in psychology and in the history of intellectual measurement. The first account of opposites being used in mental testing appeared in 1902. This initial work was authored by psychologist Edward L. Thorndike, who theorized that intelligence is the product of a large number of interconnected but nevertheless distinct mental abilities. The ability to think of words opposite to ones provided is one of those intellectual abilities.

Then, in 1925, Professor Andrew Wylie responded to what he perceived as a void in the field of mental testing. He wrote: "In spite of the very great amount of work already done, it has seemed worthwhile to the writer to carry on a somewhat extended experiment which would result in a new type of Opposites (The Alphabetical Opposites) and which would cover a wide range both in the difficulty of the stimuli and in the age and ability of the persons tested."

Professor Wylie's extensive experimentation led to a series of eight groups of words, one which you will see shortly. Each group required antonyms beginning with a specific letter of the alphabet: a, b, c, d, e, f, l, r, or t. The single-letter technique for the antonyms was suggested to Wylie by Professor Thorndike and served to limit the number of possible answers, thus increasing ease and accuracy in scoring the test.

INSTRUCTIONS

To take the Opposites Test, look at each of the words in the list that follows. Then write a word after it that means just the opposite and that begins with the letter r. *If you come to a word that you cannot respond to, go on to the next one. These three samples illustrate the correct way of responding:*

give - receive
fair - rainy
immature - ripe

There are 20 words to respond to in the test that follows. You have only two minutes to complete the test, so you must work quickly. When your time is up, stop your work and turn the page to find your score.

1. poor _rich_
2. smooth _rough_
3. fall _rise_
4. square _round_
5. forget _remember_
6. cooked _raw_
7. polite _rude_
8. unusual _____
9. unprepared _ready_
10. increase _reduce_

11. common _rare_
12. cause _____
13. flexible _rigid_
14. eager _reticent_
15. compassionate _____
16. exception _rule_
17. urban _rural_
18. avow _____
19. erect _____
20. communicative _____

SCORING

To score the test, compare your answers with those on the Scoring Key. Note that there are four columns of responses, each with a different point value. Score 3 points for words considered the best possible response. Score 2 points for words not considered the *best* response but yet of some merit. Score 1 point for words that are indirectly opposite, grammatically inappropriate, or archaic. Write your total score in the box below.

TOTAL
SCORE

INTERPRETATION

"Intelligence" in 1925 was the equivalent of what we, today, primarily regard as left-brain skills. Tests such as the popular Stanford-Binet Intelligence Scale (1916, revised 1960) defined intelligence in terms of specific school subjects, almost exclusively such left-brain tasks as arithmetic, vocabulary, and language skills. Wylie himself defined the skills involved in the Opposites Test as "English ability" but noted, perhaps somewhat facetiously, that "English ability is a term that hospitably gives shelter to a multitude of minor virtues, such as neatness and punctuality as well as skill in composition, the interpretation of difficult verbal passages, the appreciation of the style and the technique of literature, the ability to speak readily and grammatically, and the not-committing of various blunders of speech that are akin to offenses against good taste and good breeding."

Performing well on the Opposites Test requires more than a good basic vocabulary. The test forces you to recall as many antonyms of the cue word as you can and simultaneously sift through them to come up with the best one that meets the criterion of beginning with the letter *r*. For many people this involves conjuring up images of the antonyms so that they can choose those beginning with the appropriate letter.

Some occupations require high levels of skills such as those tested by the Opposites Test. Lawyers, teachers, newspaper reporters, and TV or radio broadcasters are just a few of the professionals who must employ a combination of "English ability" and speed in organizing language. People who possess high levels of such skills score above 51 on the test. Average levels of these abilities are reflected by scores between 33 and 50, while low levels of the Opposites Test's skills fall below 32. Remember that on any test requiring fast performance your score could be affected by distractions around you that prevent you from accurately answering the test questions. Combine your level of performance on the Opposites Test with those on other tests requiring speed to get an idea of how well you can work under time pressure. If you have done extremely well on this test and others tapping similar mental abilities, you may want to think about occupations that require quick thinking and accurate responses.

SCORING KEY

Points	Stimulus Word	Score 3	Score 2	Score 1	Score 0
	1. poor	rich			ripe
	2. smooth	ragged, ringed rough, ruffle	ridged	rocky	*rinkle (n.)
	3. fall	recover, right rise	rear, revive	raise, reanimate reinvigorate righten (arch. and dial.), rose	rain, reach, rebuild, remain remove, rescue, rest, retain retard, ride, river, roll, run
	4. square	ring, round			rectangle, rectangular
	5. forget	recall, recollect remember		remembered remind	recover, renew
	6. cooked	raw		rare	regular, rigid, ripe, roasted round
	7. polite	rude	rough, rowdy		rash, repulsive
	8. unusual	regular	recurrent, recurring repeated, representative routine	regularly, rule	rare, rational, real, right
	9. unprepared	ready	rehearsed	readiness responsive	raw, refined, remain remember, repaired
	10. increase	reduce, reduction relax, restrict	retard	reduced restrain	rarify, recede, recessional recided, recline, release relinquish, rescind, retract retrieve, revile
	11. common	rare, refined remarkable		refine, regal respectable, rich, royal	real, recluse, regular, reticent
	12. cause	result	reaction	repeal	reason, refuse, remains remedy, root, repair resolution
	13. flexible	rigid	reluctant, resistant resisting, resistive	resolute, resolved restrained	ramrod, reflex, reflexible restricted, rusty
	14. eager	reluctant, repressed reserved, restrained	retiring	resist, resistant resisting, reticent	refrain, regretful, resigned restive, restless, retard ridiculous, rude
	15. compassionate	relentless, remorseless ruthless		regardless, repellent	rational, refuse, remonstrate resentful, resigned, resistant resolute, restful, restraint rigorous, rough, rude
	16. exception	rule	regulation	regular, regularity	rare, rarity, reception, refuse rejection, review
	17. urban	rural	rustic	rough, (obs. sense)	resident, round
	18. avow	recant, renounce repudiate, retract		refuse, reject, renege revoke (obs.)	ratify, recognize, refrain refute, resolve, respond revenge, revise, reward
	19. erect	raze, recline, reclining recumbent		reduce, remove, round-shouldered, ruin	rear, reconstruct, revive rigid, rip, round(ed) rounded over
	20. communicative	receptive, reserved reticent, retiring		repressed, reserve retentive (obs.), retired (obs., rare) retractive	recessive, reciprocative recluse, reclusive, reflective reluctant, repulsive, resolute responsive, restful, restricted restrictive, retreating, ruptured

*While this may be regarded as a misspelling of *wrinkle* it cannot be given credit since *wrinkle* is spelled with a *w*.

15. Verbal Skills Test

Most of the information we need comes to us through the spoken and written word. We, in turn, affect those around us using our verbal skills. These skills are so essential that national policies toward education in the United States changed because of research showing that children's tested levels of verbal skills have decreased during the last two decades. School systems across the country are required to test for deficiencies in these areas and then to design and implement programs for children with such problems.

For some careers, such as teaching and writing, a high level of verbal competence is essential. In fact, most white-collar careers require good verbal skills, whether the job involves office work, research, or management. Your own level of verbal ability may have a major impact on what you can do and how far you can go in your chosen career.

The following test separates verbal skill into two of its main components: using words correctly, and understanding the relationship between words. The first part of the test requires you to complete a sentence from which one or two words have been omitted. To do well, you must look for the underlying meaning of the sentence. You must then use your vocabulary skills to discriminate among the words given as possible fill-ins.

The second half of the test deals with analogies. Each analogy expresses the relationship between the meanings and/or the usages of a pair of words. Your task is to discover that relationship and then find a second pair of words that share the same relationship. The combination of skills measured by analogies is considered essential for success in most academic programs. In fact, 100 such pairs make up the Miller Analogies Test, a test required as part of the admissions process by graduate programs across the United States.

INSTRUCTIONS

In the first section of the Verbal Skills Test you will be presented with 18 sentences, each containing one or more blank spaces. You are to choose one of the five sets of words below the sentence that best completes it.

In the second section you will be dealing with analogies. You will be presented with two words and asked to choose that one of five possible pairs that best expresses a relationship similar to that expressed by the original pair.

Before you begin the test, turn the page and remove the Answer Sheet that you will use to record your responses. When your time is up, stop your work and turn the page to find your score.

1. The _____ prowess of the pugilist
   _____fear into his opponent.
   (a) redoubtable — instilled
   (b) supernatural — propelled
   (c) probing — prevented
   (d) pedagogic — conducted
   (e) emergent — involved

2. His _____ nature will aid him in
   attaining success in this difficult job.
   (a) imitative
   (b) lackadaisical
   (c) catalytic
   (d) rotund
   (e) persevering

3. Since he is a teacher of English, we would not expect him to be guilty of a _____.
   (a) solecism
   (b) schism
   (c) stanchion
   (d) freshet
   (e) bombast

4. The servant's attitude was so _____
   that it would have been_____to
   anyone with an appreciation of sincerity.
   (a) natal — clear
   (b) hybrid — available
   (c) sycophantic — obnoxious
   (d) doleful — responsible
   (e) refulgent — candid

5. One would expect a serf to _____ to
   a lord.
   (a) arrogate
   (b) apprize
   (c) circumscribe
   (d) forage
   (e) truckle

6. Any public officer who allows bribery to flourish
   should be subject to_____.
   (a) stringency
   (b) vagary
   (c) stricture
   (d) apologue
   (e) badinage

7. The old man was so _____ that he
   refused to buy food.
   (a) parsimonious
   (b) prescient
   (c) prolix
   (d) affluent
   (e) creative

8. Our neighbor is so much disliked that we may well
   consider him a _____.
   (a) pariah
   (b) latitudinarian
   (c) calumet
   (d) cenotaph
   (e) claque

9. His_____leads me to believe that
   he cannot be_____.
   (a) mendicity — injured
   (b) mendacity — trusted
   (c) catachresis — considered
   (d) baldric — trained
   (e) blandishment — recriminated

10. Cloud formations which appear to be merely ____
    _____masses of floating atmosphere, may
    mean treacherous weather.
    (a) arboreal
    (b) chaotic
    (c) amalgamated
    (d) amorphous
    (e) insidious

11. Politics sometimes places politicians in the _____
    _____position of supporting candi-
    dates they had attacked only months before.
    (a) anomalous
    (b) piquant
    (c) succulent
    (d) strategic
    (e) embarrassing

12. Often criticism may be more effectively made
    by_____than by direct censure.
    (a) eroticism
    (b) malignity
    (c) innuendo
    (d) illusion
    (e) collusion

13. In the face of an uncooperative Congress, the
    Chief Executive may find himself _____
    to accomplish his political objectives.
    (a) impotent
    (b) ambulant
    (c) neutral
    (d) contingent
    (e) equipped

14. A policy of noncooperation can be a certain
    method of_____coworkers.
    (a) abominating
    (b) alienating
    (c) aborting
    (d) evacuating
    (e) emanating

15. The economic stability of nations and continents
    is often affected by the abundance or
    _____of precipitation.
    (a) force
    (b) condensation
    (c) rainfall
    (d) dearth
    (e) allusion

16. Many of America's quaint customs, spawned by
    the exigencies of pioneer days, have fallen in-
    to_____.
    (a) oblivion
    (b) desuetude
    (c) concatenation
    (d) chasm
    (e) favor

110

ANSWER SHEET

15. Verbal Skills Test

	a	b	c	d	e		a	b	c	d	e
1.	0	0	0	0	0	19.	0	0	0	0	0
2.	0	0	0	0	0	20.	0	0	0	0	0
3.	0	0	0	0	0	21.	0	0	0	0	0
4.	0	0	0	0	0	22.	0	0	0	0	0
5.	0	0	0	0	0	23.	0	0	0	0	0
6.	0	0	0	0	0	24.	0	0	0	0	0
7.	0	0	0	0	0	25.	0	0	0	0	0
8.	0	0	0	0	0	26.	0	0	0	0	0
9.	0	0	0	0	0	27.	0	0	0	0	0
10.	0	0	0	0	0	28.	0	0	0	0	0
11.	0	0	0	0	0	29.	0	0	0	0	0
12.	0	0	0	0	0	30.	0	0	0	0	0
13.	0	0	0	0	0	31.	0	0	0	0	0
14.	0	0	0	0	0	32.	0	0	0	0	0
15.	0	0	0	0	0	33.	0	0	0	0	0
16.	0	0	0	0	0	34.	0	0	0	0	0
17.	0	0	0	0	0	35.	0	0	0	0	0
18.	0	0	0	0	0	36.	0	0	0	0	0

(Tear Out)

ANSWER SHEET

15. Verbal Skills Test

	a	b	c	d	e			a	b	c	d	e
1.	0	0	0	0	0		19.	0	0	0	0	0
2.	0	0	0	0	0		20.	0	0	0	0	0
3.	0	0	0	0	0		21.	0	0	0	0	0
4.	0	0	0	0	0		22.	0	0	0	0	0
5.	0	0	0	0	0		23.	0	0	0	0	0
6.	0	0	0	0	0		24.	0	0	0	0	0
7.	0	0	0	0	0		25.	0	0	0	0	0
8.	0	0	0	0	0		26.	0	0	0	0	0
9.	0	0	0	0	0		27.	0	0	0	0	0
10.	0	0	0	0	0		28.	0	0	0	0	0
11.	0	0	0	0	0		29.	0	0	0	0	0
12.	0	0	0	0	0		30.	0	0	0	0	0
13.	0	0	0	0	0		31.	0	0	0	0	0
14.	0	0	0	0	0		32.	0	0	0	0	0
15.	0	0	0	0	0		33.	0	0	0	0	0
16.	0	0	0	0	0		34.	0	0	0	0	0
17.	0	0	0	0	0		35.	0	0	0	0	0
18.	0	0	0	0	0		36.	0	0	0	0	0

(Tear Out)

17. When the mind imagines things which _____ or hinder physical reaction, it endeavors to suppress them as much as possible.
    (a) diminish
    (b) portray
    (c) default
    (d) affront
    (e) fluctuate

18. Some works of literature hold the interest to the very last page, but others serve only as a _____, to be kept handily at a bedside table.
    (a) fluvial
    (b) deodorant
    (c) soporific
    (d) epigram
    (e) portend

In the items below, choose the lettered pair that expresses a relationship most similar to that expressed by the capitalized pair.

---

19. AFFIRM : HINT ::
    (a) say : deny
    (b) assert : convince
    (c) confirm : reject
    (d) charge : insinuate
    (e) state : relate

20. THROW : BALL ::
    (a) kill : bullet
    (b) shoot : gun
    (c) question : answer
    (d) hit : run
    (e) stab : knife

21. SPEEDY : GREYHOUND ::
    (a) innocent : lamb
    (b) animate : animal
    (c) voracious : tiger
    (d) clever : fox
    (e) sluggish : sloth

22. TRIANGLE : PYRAMID ::
    (a) cone : circle
    (b) corner : angle
    (c) tube : cylinder
    (d) pentagon : quadrilateral
    (e) square : cube

23. CIRCLE : SPHERE ::
    (a) square : triangle
    (b) balloon : jet plane
    (c) heaven : hell
    (d) wheel : orange
    (e) pill : drop

24. OPEN : SECRETIVE ::
    (a) mystery : detective
    (b) tunnel : toll
    (c) forthright : snide
    (d) better : best
    (e) gun : mask

25. 36 : 4 ::
    (a) 3 : 27
    (b) 9 : 1
    (c) 12 : 4
    (d) 49 : 7
    (e) 5 : 2

26. IMPEACH : DISMISS ::
    (a) arraign : convict
    (b) exonerate : charge
    (c) imprison : jail
    (d) plant : reap
    (e) president : Johnson

27. GERM : DISEASE ::
    (a) trichinosis : pork
    (b) men : woman
    (c) doctor : medicine
    (d) war : destruction
    (e) biologist : cell

28. PLUTOCRACY : WEALTHY ::
    (a) autocracy : group
    (b) democracy : people
    (c) hierarchy : government
    (d) oligarchy : tyrant
    (e) theocracy : demagogue

29. HANDCUFFS : ROBBER ::
    (a) leash : dog
    (b) rope : tie
    (c) shoes : feet
    (d) law : restriction
    (e) paper : kite

30. FRIDAY : TUESDAY ::
    (a) 3:00 A.M. : 11:00 A.M.
    (b) 6:00 P.M. : 10:00 A.M.
    (c) 7:00 P.M. : 11:00 P.M.
    (d) 5:00 A.M. : 9:00 P.M.
    (e) 12:00 A.M. : 12:00 P.M.

31. TELEPHONE : LETTER ::
    (a) loudspeaker : microphone
    (b) phonograph : manuscript
    (c) telegraph : telephone
    (d) sound : sight
    (e) brush : canvas

32. IMMIGRATION : ENTRANCE ::
    (a) native : foreigner
    (b) emigration : departure
    (c) file : knife
    (d) travel : alien
    (e) nest : bird

33. HOTEL : SHELTER ::
    (a) bed : pillow
    (b) boat : transportation
    (c) train : ride
    (d) restaurant : drink
    (e) home : recuperation

34. URGE : INSIST ::
    (a) request : hound
    (b) plead : beg
    (c) refuse : deny
    (d) scourge : purge
    (e) finish : begin

35. ASCETIC : LUXURY ::
    (a) misogynist : women
    (b) philosopher : knowledge
    (c) capitalist : industry
    (d) general : victory
    (e) teacher : blackboard

36. DISHONESTY : DISTRUST ::
    (a) violin : bow
    (b) hand : paper
    (c) money : thief
    (d) carelessness : accident
    (e) stealing : murder

SCORING

To find your score, compare your responses on the Answer Sheet to those on the Scoring Key below. Give yourself 1 point for each correct answer and write the total in the box below. For a more detailed look at the answers, see the Explanatory Answers.

TOTAL
SCORE

SCORING KEY

1.	a	19.	d
2.	e	20.	b
3.	a	21.	e
4.	c	22.	e
5.	e	23.	d
6.	c	24.	c
7.	a	25.	b
8.	a	26.	a
9.	b	27.	d
10.	d	28.	b
11.	a	29.	a
12.	c	30.	b
13.	a	31.	d
14.	b	32.	b
15.	d	33.	b
16.	b	34.	a
17.	a	35.	a
18.	c	36.	d

INTERPRETATION

The Verbal Skills Test measures your knowledge of words and your ability to see relationships between meanings and uses of words. The key to doing well in the sentence-completion part of the test is the ability to use a word in context, thus understanding the intent of the sentence.

The key to answering analogy questions well is the ability to analyze the relationship between pairs of words. A large vocabulary does help, however, since not knowing a word makes the next step impossible.

A strong performance on the Verbal Skills Test is represented by a score of 30 to 36. If you scored here, you are no doubt aware of your verbal skills since such tasks are most likely enjoyable for you. (We tend to occupy our time with those things we're good at.) A large vocabulary, combined with reasoning ability, is useful for careers in publishing, law, politics, advertising, or journalism.

A score of 23 to 29 falls into the average level of performance on this test. Your first step should be to examine the pattern of your correct answers to see if more occurred in one half of the test than in the other. If that's the case, you would probably benefit from practice in your weaker skill area, since your basic verbal skills may be greater than your score indicates.

Chances are you didn't score in the range indicating a weak level of verbal ability, below 12. People who are not at least average in verbal skills probably do not find books like *The Brain Game* interesting or worthwhile.

EXPLANATORY ANSWERS

1. (a). The powers of a pugilist (prizefighter) could hardly be called supernatural (b) or pedagogic (d). To say that he prevented (c) or involved (e) fear into his opponent would be incorrect usage. Therefore, *redoubtable* (formidable) — *instilled* (a) is the best completion.

2. (e). Of the options given, a persevering nature is the personal attribute which would best equip a person to perform a difficult job.

3. (a). *Solecism* (an error in speech or writing) is the word which best fits the sentence.

4. (c). A sycophantic (fawning, flattering) attitude would be obnoxious to one with an appreciation of sincerity.

5. (e). *Truckle* (to act in a subservient manner) is the best completion.

6. (c). *Stricture* (censure) is the word which best completes the sentence.

7. (a). A person who is parsimonious (stingy) could be so to such a degree that he would refuse to buy food.

8. (a). One who is intensely disliked could be considered a pariah.

9. (b). A person who possessed the quality of mendacity (falsehood) would not be trusted.

10. (d). *Amorphous* (shapeless) is the best completion.

11. (a). *Anomalous* (inconsistent, irregular) is the word which would best describe the action of a politician who endorsed a candidate whom he had attacked just two months before.

12. (c). *Innuendo* (indirect suggestion) is the opposite of *direct criticism* and hence the best completion.

13. (a). Given the circumstances described in the sentence, the Chief Executive might find himself impotent or unable to accomplish that which he wishes to do.

14. (b). *Alienate* (to make unfriendly, hostile, or indifferent) is the word which best fits the meaning of the sentence.

15. (d). *Dearth* (lack or scarcity) is the opposite of *abundance* and is therefore the word which best completes the sentence.

16. (b). *Desuetude* (disuse) is the word which best fits the meaning of the sentence.

17. (a). *Diminish* is the word closest in meaning to *hinder* and hence the best completion.

18. (c). A book that acts as a soporific (something which induces sleep) would be the opposite of a book which holds one's interest to the last page.

19. (d). When you affirm, you are direct; when you hint, you are indirect. When you charge, you are direct; when you insinuate, you are indirect.

20. (b). One throws a ball and one shoots a gun.

21. (e). In terms of rate of movement, a greyhound is proverbially speedy; on the other hand, a sloth is proverbially sluggish.

22. (e). A triangle is a plane figure; a pyramid is a solid figure having triangles for faces. A square is a plane figure; a cube is a solid figure having squares for faces.

23. (d). All four are round: circle, sphere, wheel, and orange.

24. (c). *Open* is the opposite of *secretive*; *forthright* is the opposite of *snide*.

25. (b). $36 = 9 \times 4$; $9 = 9 \times 1$.

26. (a). To impeach is to charge or challenge; if the impeachment proceedings are successful, the charged person is dismissed. To arraign is to call into court as a result of accusation; if the accusation is proved correct, the arraigned person is convicted.

27. (d). A germ often causes disease; a war often causes destruction.

28. (b). Plutocracy is government by the wealthy; democracy is government by the people.

29. (a). Handcuffs are used to restrain a robber; a leash is used to restrain a dog.

30. (b). Friday comes later in the week than Tuesday; 6:00 P.M. comes later in the day than 10:00 A.M.

31. (d). A telephone communicates by means of sound; a letter communicates by sight.

32. (b). To immigrate is to enter a new country; to emigrate is to depart from one's own country.

33. (b). A hotel provides shelter; a boat provides transportation.

34. (a). To urge is milder than to insist; to request is milder than to hound.

35. (a). An ascetic objects to and avoids luxury; a misogynist objects to and avoids women.

36. (d). Dishonesty can cause distrust; carelessness can cause an accident.

16. Block-Counting and Analysis Test

by David R. Turner

Each world war has created a need for a psychological test. World War I required the development of the Woodsworth Personal Data Sheet in 1918 to help the Army screen out "undesirable" inductees. World War II created a need for a general intelligence test that could be given to hundreds of men simultaneously. The result was the Army General Classification Test (AGCT), which was administered to more than 12 million men during the war.

The test that follows is not in *The Brain Game* to prepare you for the armed forces. We have included these items because one third of the AGCT items are different from the verbal and quantitative items found in typical intelligence tests. The block-counting and analysis problems that follow either come from or were patterned after those in the AGCT. They are designed to measure the spatial factor in general intelligence. In essence, they ask, "How well can you create a mental image of a three-dimensional object from a two-dimensional drawing and then apply problem-solving skills to it?" In effect, the test asks you to combine the spatial skills from your brain's right hemisphere with the linear counting-and-analysis skills from the left hemisphere. The test will force you to visualize and count quickly. Charge ahead.

INSTRUCTIONS

In the Block-Counting and Analysis Test you will be presented with 24 piles of blocks. Your task is to count the number of blocks in each pile. For example, count the blocks below.

The right number is four blocks. Only three blocks would be shown in the test, but here we have revealed the hidden block that supports the structure.

Next look at the problem below.

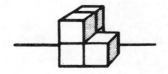

The correct answer is five blocks. As you take the test, keep in mind that every block is the same size and shape. Do not forget to count the hidden blocks.

Before you begin the test, tear out the Answer Sheet on the facing page, and use it to record your responses. There is space for your computations as well. You will have only 15 minutes in which to complete the test so you must work quickly. When your time is up, stop your work and turn the page to find your score.

ANSWER SHEET

16. Block-Counting and Analysis Test

1. _____   13. _____
2. _____   14. _____
3. _____   15. _____
4. _____   16. _____
5. _____   17. _____
6. _____   18. _____
7. _____   19. _____
8. _____   20. _____
9. _____   21. _____
10. _____   22. _____
11. _____   23. _____
12. _____   24. _____

NOTES

ANSWER SHEET

16. Block-Counting and Analysis Test

1. _32_
2. _35_
3. _40_ x
4. _56_
5. _24_
6. _38_
7. _49_
8. _48_
9. _15_ x
10. _59_
11. _40_
12. _95_

13. _59_
14. _67_ x
15. _17_
16. _33_ x
17. _24_
18. _112_
19. _44_ x
20. _57_ x
21. _60_ x
22. _58_
23. _56_ x
24. _97_ x

NOTES

45
88
15
7
95

M
85
14
19
67

18
9
72

72
32
8
112

(Tear Out)

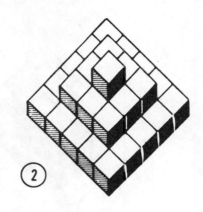

(5)

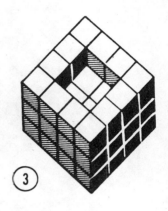

(4)

(3)

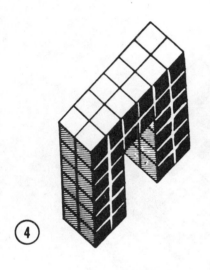

(7)

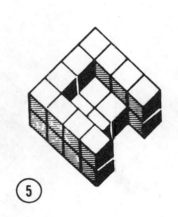

(6)

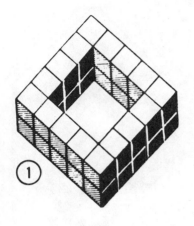

(8)

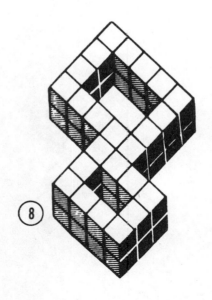

(2)

(1)

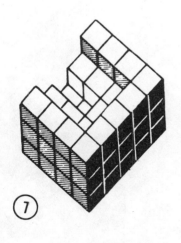

(9)

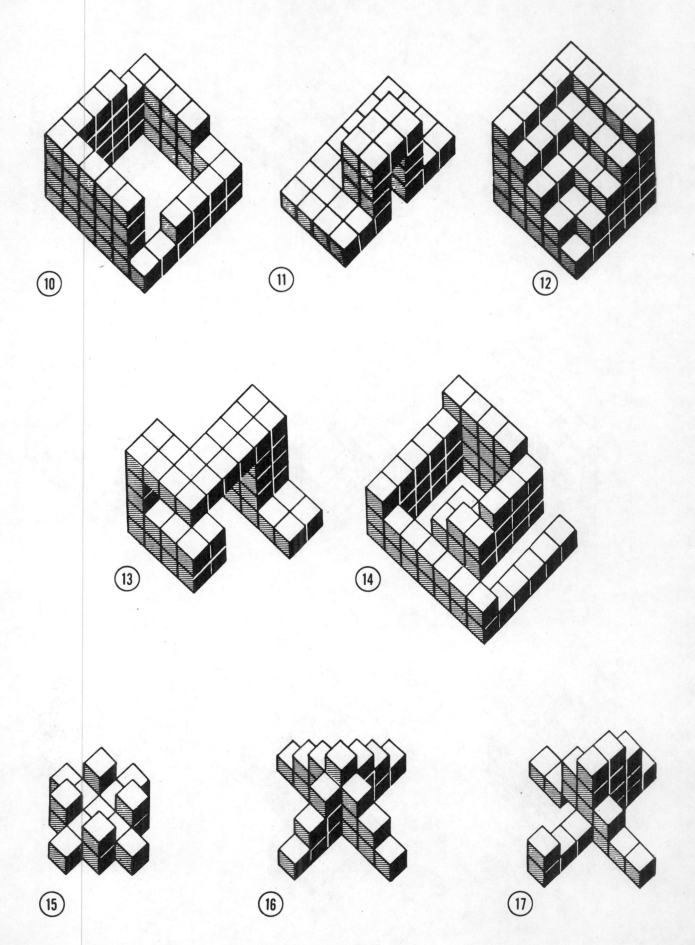

⑩   ⑪   ⑫

⑬   ⑭

⑮   ⑯   ⑰

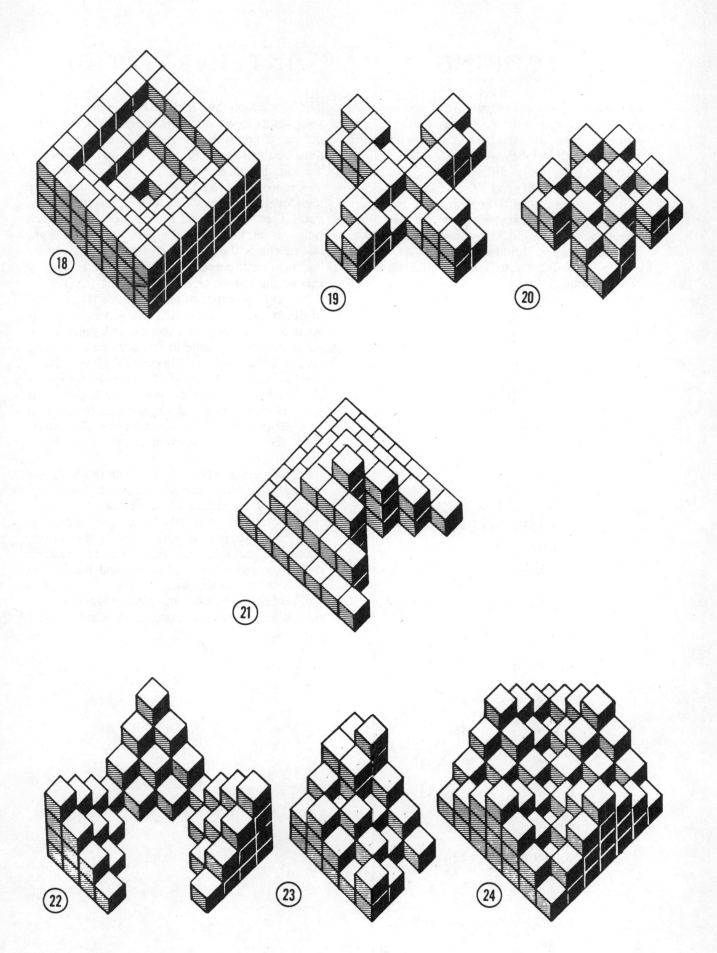

SCORING

To find your score, compare your responses on the Answer Sheet to the Scoring Key below. Give yourself 1 point for each correct answer and write the total in the box below.

Some of the more difficult problems are the arches in items 4, 11, and 17. The upper blocks in item 13 are presumably kept in place by a very strong cement. The answer given for item 9 assumes there is no block in the northern corner. And on item 24 you will have the correct answer if you realized that there is at least one block in every column.

TOTAL
SCORE

SCORING KEY

1.	32	13.	56
2.	35	14.	63 or 64
3.	44	15.	17
4.	56	16.	28
5.	24	17.	24
6.	38	18.	112
7.	49	19.	46
8.	48	20.	32
9.	14	21.	70
10.	59	22.	58
11.	40	23.	47
12.	95	24.	105

INTERPRETATION

The Block-Counting and Analysis Test measures your ability to visualize and analyze what you cannot see. To do well with these "little boxes," you must be able to mentally walk around the drawing, counting blocks that are hidden from your view.

A score of 18 to 24 on this test indicates a very high level of spatial ability. It suggests that you, if you scored here, would probably do well in such fields as architecture, drafting, interior design, and mechanical engineering. Research has shown that dentistry, carpentry, and surgery frequently rely on the same type of spatial ability.

The average range of ability on this test, a score of 10 to 17, probably indicates a person who is good at spatial tasks in a specific area, such as the accountant who is able to visualize on charts and graphs a client's future finances. Or it may mean that you have only partially developed your spatial abilities and could refine them to a higher level with more practice and experience. If you find yourself playing the role of a weekend architect, think about how courses in design might affect your career.

To the person who scored low on this test, that is, below 9, an architect's blueprints for a new building or an engineer's design for a new car would probably look like little more than flat drawings on paper. If you scored in this range, you are probably more comfortable dealing with real objects that you can grasp and manipulate than with two-dimensional representations. You will probably find that your occupation and interests do not require a strong emphasis on spatial analysis.

17. Reading Comprehension Test

Reading has always been one of the most basic and essential of intellectual abilities. "Reading," in the words of Sir Francis Bacon, "maketh a full man" (and he would no doubt add "or woman or child" if he were alive today). The ability to read quickly and yet comprehend well plays an important role in our survival — from reading street signs and basic instructions when we are young, to reading newspapers, magazines, documents, and books as we mature.

Skill in reading quickly and comprehending in depth what was read is required by people working as newspaper reporters, editors, secretaries, researchers, teachers, and lawyers. Research has shown that, up to a point, people who read quickly usually comprehend best. The theory is that deeper concentration is required for rapid reading. The questions that follow will test your ability to combine reading speed and comprehension. Read on.

INSTRUCTIONS

In the Reading Comprehension Test, you will be presented with four reading passages. Read each passage and answer the accompanying questions, basing your answers on what is stated or implied in the passage.

Before you begin the test, turn the page and tear out the Answer Sheet that you will use to record your answers. Give yourself 20 minutes to complete the test. When your time is up, stop your work and turn the page to find your score.

© 1980 Arco Publishing, Inc. From The Graduate Record Examination Aptitude Test by the Arco Editorial Board.

If a man were called to fix the period in the history of the world during which the condition of the human race was most happy and prosperous, he would, without hesitation, name that which elapsed from the death of Domitian to the accession of Commodus [A.D. 96 – 180]. The vast extent of the Roman Empire was governed by absolute power, under the guidance of virtue and wisdom. The armies were restrained by the firm but gentle hand of four successive emperors, whose characters and authority commanded involuntary respect. The forms of the civil administration were carefully preserved by Nerva, Trajan, Hadrian, and the Antonines, who delighted in the image of liberty, and were pleased with considering themselves as the accountable ministers of the laws. Such princes deserved the honor of restoring the republic, had the Romans of their days been capable of enjoying a rational freedom.

The labors of these monarchs were overpaid by the immense reward that inseparably waited on their success: by the honest pride of virtue, and by the exquisite delight of beholding the general happiness of which they were the authors. A just, but melancholy reflection embittered, however, the noblest of human enjoyments. They must often

123

have recollected the instability of a happiness which depended on the character of a single man. The fatal moment was perhaps approaching, when some licentious youth, or some jealous tyrant, would abuse, to the destruction, that absolute power, which they had exerted for the benefit of their people. The ideal restraints of the Senate and the laws might serve to display the virtues, but could never correct the vices, of the emperor. The military force was a blind and irresistible instrument of oppression; and the corruption of Roman manners would always supply flatterers eager to applaud, and ministers prepared to serve, the fear or the avarice, the lust or the cruelty, of their masters.

These gloomy apprehensions had been already justified by the experience of the Romans. The annals of the emperors exhibit a strong and various picture of human nature, which we should vainly seek among the mixed and doubtful characters of modern history. In the conduct of those monarchs we may trace the utmost lines of vice and virtue: the most exalted perfection, and the meanest degeneracy of our own species. The golden age of Trajan and the Antonines had been preceded by an age of iron. It is almost superfluous to enumerate the unworthy successors of Augustus. Their unparalleled vices, and the splendid theater on which they were acted, have saved them from oblivion. The dark unrelenting Tiberius, the furious Caligula, the feeble Claudius, the profligate and cruel Nero, the beastly Vitellius, and the timid inhuman Domitian are condemned to everlasting infamy. During fourscore years (excepting only the short and doubtful respite of Vespasian's reign) Rome groaned beneath an unremitting tyranny, which exterminated the ancient families of the republic, and was fatal to almost every virtue and every talent that arose in that unhappy period.

1. The emperor group which is spoken of favorably includes
    (a) Trajan, Caligula, Hadrian
    (b) the Antonines, Vespasian, Domitian
    (c) Nerva, Claudius, Vitellius
    (c) Claudius, Caligula, the Antonines
    (e) Nerva, Trajan, Hadrian

2. The period during which the Roman Empire showed greatest stability was the
    (a) second century B.C.
    (b) first century B.C.
    (c) second century A.D.
    (c) first century A.D.
    (e) none of the above

3. Which of the following can be inferred about the Roman emperors?
    (a) They all had trouble controlling the military.
    (b) Some had doubts about the virtue of one-man rule.
    (c) Most of them were superior to leaders in other countries.
    (d) The later Roman emperors built upon the success of earlier ones.
    (e) They each in his own way worked for the happiness of all citizens.

4. According to the author, Roman emperors are unique in that
    (a) they represent greater variety of moral conduct than any other group of leaders
    (b) they are unmatched for their cruelty
    (c) their life spans were shorter than those of any other group of rulers
    (d) they were the most capable leaders in all history
    (e) they encouraged the building of roads and temples

5. It can be inferred that the author believes which of the following about dictatorial government of the type found in ancient Rome?
    I. It caused great hardship.
    II. It was the best possible form of government, given the circumstances.
    III. It created the time of greatest human happiness.

    (a) I only
    (b) II only
    (c) I and III only
    (d) II and III only
    (e) I, II, and III

6. According to the passage, Vespasian's reign can best be characterized as
    (a) violent
    (b) prosperous
    (c) victorious
    (d) democratic
    (e) short

ANSWER SHEET

17. Reading Comprehension Test

	a	b	c	d	e			a	b	c	d	e
1.	0	0	0	0	0		13.	0	0	0	0	0
2.	0	0	0	0	0		14.	0	0	0	0	0
3.	0	0	0	0	0		15.	0	0	0	0	0
4.	0	0	0	0	0		16.	0	0	0	0	0
5.	0	0	0	0	0		17.	0	0	0	0	0
6.	0	0	0	0	0		18.	0	0	0	0	0
7.	0	0	0	0	0		19.	0	0	0	0	0
8.	0	0	0	0	0		20.	0	0	0	0	0
9.	0	0	0	0	0		21.	0	0	0	0	0
10.	0	0	0	0	0		22.	0	0	0	0	0
11.	0	0	0	0	0		23.	0	0	0	0	0
12.	0	0	0	0	0		24.	0	0	0	0	0

NOTES

(Tear Out)

ANSWER SHEET

17. Reading Comprehension Test

	a	b	c	d	e			a	b	c	d	e
1.	0	0	0	0	0		13.	0	0	0	0	0
2.	0	0	0	0	0		14.	0	0	0	0	0
3.	0	0	0	0	0		15.	0	0	0	0	0
4.	0	0	0	0	0		16.	0	0	0	0	0
5.	0	0	0	0	0		17.	0	0	0	0	0
6.	0	0	0	0	0		18.	0	0	0	0	0
7.	0	0	0	0	0		19.	0	0	0	0	0
8.	0	0	0	0	0		20.	0	0	0	0	0
9.	0	0	0	0	0		21.	0	0	0	0	0
10.	0	0	0	0	0		22.	0	0	0	0	0
11.	0	0	0	0	0		23.	0	0	0	0	0
12.	0	0	0	0	0		24.	0	0	0	0	0

NOTES

(Tear Out)

Do students learn from programmed instruction? The research leaves us in no doubt of this. They do, indeed, learn. They learn from linear programs, from branching programs built on the Skinnerian model, from scrambled books of the Crowder type, from Pressey review tests with immediate knowledge of results, from programs on machines or programs in texts. Many kinds of students learn — college, high school, secondary, primary, preschool, adult, professional, laboring, clerical, military, deaf, retarded, imprisoned — every kind of student that programs have been tried on. Using programs, these students are able to learn mathematics and science at different levels, foreign languages, correct English, the details of the U.S. Constitution, spelling, electronics, computer science, psychology, statistics, business skills, reading skills, instrument flying rules, and many other subjects. The limits of the topics which can be studied efficiently by means of programs are not yet known.

For each of the kinds of subject matter and the kinds of student mentioned above, experiments have demonstrated that a considerable amount of learning can be derived from programs; this learning has been measured either by comparing pre- and post-tests or the time and trials needed to reach a set criterion of performance. But the question of how well students learn from programs, as compared to how well they learn from other kinds of instruction, we cannot answer quite so confidently.

Experimental psychologists typically do not take very seriously the evaluative experiments in which learning from programs is compared with learning from conventional teaching. Such experiments are doubtless useful, they say, for school administrators or teachers to prove to themselves (or their boards of education) that programs work. But whereas one can describe fairly well the characteristics of a program, can one describe the characteristics of a classroom teaching situation so that the result of the comparison will have any generality? What kind of teacher is being compared to what kind of program? Furthermore, these early evaluative experiments with programs are likely to suffer from the Hawthorne effect; that is to say, students are in the spotlight when testing something new, and are challenged to do well. It is very hard to make allowance for this effect. Therefore, the evaluative tests may be useful administratively, say many of the experimenters, but do not contribute much to science, and should properly be kept for private use.

These objections are well taken. And yet, do they justify us in ignoring the evaluative studies? The great strength of a program is that it permits the student to learn efficiently by himself. Is it not therefore important to know how many and what kind of skills, concepts, insights, or attitudes he can learn by himself from a program as compared to what he can learn from a teacher? Admittedly, this is a very difficult and complex research problem, but that should not keep us from trying to solve it.

7. The author mentions the "Hawthorne effect" to illustrate a
   (a) type of programmed learning device
   (b) way programmed learning devices can be used for instruction
   (c) difficulty in effectively evaluating programmed learning material
   (d) principle used in effective classroom teaching
   (e) way to apply programmed learning to classroom situations

8. Of the following, the most appropriate title for the passage would be
   (a) "The History of Programmed Learning Devices"
   (b) "How to Use Programmed Teaching Machines in the Classroom"
   (c) "How Effective Is Programmed Instruction?"
   (d) "Subjects We Can Teach Ourselves Through Programmed Learning"
   (e) "Types of Programmed Learning Devices in Common Use Today"

9. According to the passage, experimental psychologists typically view the results of experiments comparing programmed instruction to conventional teaching methods with
   (a) skepticism
   (b) distaste
   (c) great interest
   (d) complete acceptance
   (e) extreme annoyance

10. According to the passage, the great strength of programmed instruction is that the student can learn
    (a) to obtain better grades than he otherwise might
    (b) faster than with other methods
    (c) more difficult material than with other methods
    (d) a variety of skills at the same time
    (e) efficiently by himself

11. The author's main purpose is to point out that programmed instruction
    (a) deserves further investigation
    (b) is a superior method of teaching
    (c) comes in a variety of forms
    (d) is criticized by educators
    (e) is the teaching method that is most effective

12. According to the passage, which of the following experimental variables is the most difficult to evaluate in experiments comparing programmed instruction to classroom teaching?
    (a) variability among students
    (b) variability among types of programmed methods
    (c) variability among experimental psychologists
    (d) variability among classroom teachers
    (e) variability among school administrators

"I have considered the structure of all volant animals, and find the folding continuity of the bat's wings most easily accommodated to the human form. Upon this model I shall begin my task tomorrow, and in a year expect to tower into the air beyond the malice or pursuit of man. But I will work only on this condition, that the art shall not be divulged, and that you shall not require me to make wings for any but ourselves."

"Why," said Rasselas, "should you envy others so great an advantage? All skill ought to be exerted for universal good; every man has owed much to others, and ought to repay the kindness that he has received."

"If men were all virtuous," returned the artist, "I should with great alacrity teach them all to fly. But what would be the security of the good, if the bad could at pleasure invade them from the sky? Against an army sailing through the clouds neither wall, nor mountains, nor seas could afford any security. A flight of northern savages might hover in the wind, and light at once with irresistible violence upon the capital of a fruitful region that was rolling under them. Even this valley, the retreat of princes, the abode of happiness, might be violated by the sudden descent of some of the naked nations that swarm on the coast of the southern sea."

13. The word *volant*, according to the context, means
    (a) crawling
    (b) violent
    (c) carnivorous
    (d) ferocious
    (e) flying

14. The point of view of Rasselas is one that encourages
    (a) helping others
    (b) military victory
    (c) intellectual pursuits
    (d) artistic endeavors
    (e) protecting one's property

15. The person whom Rasselas is speaking to is
    (a) a tailor
    (b) a gambler
    (c) a bat
    (d) an artist
    (e) a biologist

16. The attitude of the person giving his point of view is one of
    (a) optimism
    (b) sprightliness
    (c) distrust
    (d) innocence
    (e) sarcasm

17. The literary form which the selection most nearly resembles is
    (a) fable
    (b) sonnet
    (c) Platonic dialogue
    (d) *terza rima*
    (e) epic

18. Armed conflict, according to the passage, can be prevented by
    (a) arming for defense
    (b) eliminating evil tendencies
    (c) resorting to stratagem
    (d) establishing firm controls
    (e) letting the intellectuals govern

Shams and delusions are esteemed for soundest truths, while reality is fabulous. If men would steadily observe realities only, and not allow themselves to be deluded, life, to compare it with such things as we know, would be like a fairy tale and *The Arabian Nights' Entertainments.* If we respected only what is inevitable and has a right to be, music and poetry would resound along the streets. When we are unhurried and wise, we perceive that only great and worthy things have any permanent and absolute existence — that petty fears and petty pleasures are but the shadow of the reality. This is always exhilarating and sublime. By closing the eyes and slumbering, and consenting to be deceived by shows, men establish and confirm their daily life of routine and habit everywhere, which still is built on purely illusory foundations. Children, who play life, discern its true law and relations more clearly than men, who fail to live it worthily, but who think that they are wiser by experience, that is, by failure. I have read in a Hindu book that "there was a king's son, who, being expelled in infancy from his native city, was brought up by a forester, and, growing up to maturity in that state, imagined himself to belong to the barbarous race with which he lived. One of his father's ministers, having discovered him, revealed to him what he was, and the misconception of his character was removed, and he knew himself to be a prince. So soul," continues the Hindu philosopher, "from the circumstances in which it is placed, mistakes its own character, until the truth is revealed to it by some holy teacher, and then it knows itself to be *Brahme.*" We think that that *is* which *appears* to be. If a man should give us an account of the realities he beheld, we should not recognize the place in his description. Look at a meetinghouse, or a courthouse, or a jail, or a shop, or a dwelling house, and say what that thing really is before a true gaze, and they would all go to pieces in your account of them. Men esteem truth remote, in the outskirts of the system, behind the farthest star, before Adam and after the last man. In eternity there is indeed something true and sublime. But all these times and places and occasions are now and here. God himself culminates in the present moment, and will never be more divine in the lapse of all ages. And we are enabled to apprehend at all what is sublime and noble only by the perpetual instilling and drenching of the reality that surrounds us. The universe constantly and obediently answers to our conceptions; whether we travel fast or slow, the track is laid for us. Let us spend our lives in conceiving then. The poet or the artist never yet had so fair and noble a design but some of his posterity at least could accomplish it.

19. The writer's attitude toward the arts is one of
    (a) indifference
    (b) suspicion
    (c) admiration
    (d) repulsion
    (e) flippancy

20. The author believes that a child
    (a) should practice what the Hindus preach
    (b) frequently faces reality better than grown-ups do
    (c) prefers to be a barbarian rather than be a prince
    (d) hardly ever knows his true origin
    (e) is incapable of appreciating the arts

21. The passage implies that human beings
    (a) cannot distinguish the true from the untrue
    (b) are immoral if they are lazy
    (c) should be bold and fearless
    (d) believe in fairy tales
    (e) have progressed culturally throughout history

22. The word *fabulous* in the second line means
    (a) wonderful
    (b) delicious
    (c) birdlike
    (d) incomprehensible
    (e) nonexistent

23. The author is primarily concerned with urging the reader to
    (a) meditate on the meaninglessness of the present
    (b) look to the future for enlightenment
    (c) appraise the present for its true value
    (d) honor the wisdom of past ages
    (e) spend more time in leisure activities

24. The passage is primarily concerned with problems of
    (a) history and economics
    (b) society and population
    (c) biology and physics
    (d) theology and philosophy
    (e) music and art

SCORING

To find your score, compare your responses on the Answer Sheet to those on the Scoring Key below. Give yourself 1 point for each correct answer and write your total in the box below. For a more complete look at the answers, see the Explanatory Answers.

TOTAL
SCORE

SCORING KEY

1.	e	13.	e
2.	c	14.	a
3.	b	15.	d
4.	a	16.	c
5.	e	17.	c
6.	e	18.	d
7.	c	19.	c
8.	c	20.	b
9.	a	21.	a
10.	e	22.	e
11.	a	23.	c
12.	d	24.	d

INTERPRETATION

Now you can relax and read this section in depth (or skim it, depending on how well you scored). First, let us point out that a score of 17 to 24 shows a strong ability in reading comprehension, 10 to 16 is an average level, and 0 to 9 indicates weakness in combining reading speed with comprehension.

A high level of reading comprehension suggests that you have skill in pulling the central ideas from a series of sentences. This ability probably benefits your work efficiency and broadens what you can do for relaxation and personal gains at home. Even if your present work requires little in the way of reading speed, possessing such skill increases your job opportunities.

If you scored lower on this test than you expected, you may have only now learned how poorly you read. Research has suggested that many poor readers are unaware of how little speed and comprehension they have. Remember, however, that you can upgrade your level of reading ability.

In most reading programs, the first step in increasing your skills is to develop a plan. One of the major goals in your plan should be to learn to read as the author tried to write — taking in a series of ideas rather than a large number of words placed side by side. You will need to increase the number of words that your eyes take in with one look. You will also need to become aware of any vocalizing you do — saying the words silently to yourself as you read them.

Many people worry that they will not understand what they read if they start to read faster. Not true. Your comprehension will keep pace with your speed. Work on increasing your vocabulary — particularly if other tests in *The Brain Game* suggest you can use improvement in this area. In addition, develop a technique for extracting the central thought from each paragraph. Usually a topic sentence in the paragraph can be identified as expressing the main point.

There are many other techniques that you can use for increasing both reading speed and comprehension. Many programs specifically designed to evaluate and improve your reading skills are available. Exploring one of these programs may be one of the most direct ways you could help yourself to improve your overall intellectual skills.

EXPLANATORY ANSWERS

1. (e). The passage states: "The forms of civil administration were carefully preserved by Nerva, Trajan, Hadrian, and the Antonines, who delighted in the image of liberty," etc. Also Caligula, Claudius, and Domitian, whose names appear in all the other options, are all spoken of unfavorably.

2. (c). The period which the passage praises for its stability and which constitutes the prime subject of the passage is the period between A.D. 96 and 180, which is mainly the second century A.D.

3. (b). The passage states: "They (the emperors) must often have recollected the instability of a happiness which depended on the character of a single man."

4. (a). The passage states: "The annals of the emperors exhibit a strong and various picture of human nature, which we should vainly seek among the mixed and doubtful characters of modern history. In the conduct of these monarchs we may trace the utmost lines of vice and virtue . . . ."

5. (e). Although apparently mutually contradictory, all of the beliefs listed can be attributed to the author. He states that the Romans in the days of Nerva, Trajan, Hadrian, and the Antonines were not "capable of enjoying a rational freedom," and, therefore, that a dictatorial form of government was best. Hence, statement II can be attributed to the author. He also calls the reigns of the above-mentioned emperors "the period in the history of the world during which the condition of the human race was most happy and prosperous." Therefore, statement III can be attributed to him as well. Later in the passage, however, the author discussed the abuses of absolute power practiced by some of the earlier emperors, referring to their reigns as "that unhappy period." Hence, statement I can also be attributed to the author.

6. (e). The passage refers to "the short and doubtful respite of Vespasian's reign."

7. (c). The passage states: "Furthermore, these really evaluative experiments with programs are likely to suffer from the Hawthorne effect . . . "

8. (c). This is the question asked by the very first sentence of the passage. The passage goes on to discuss those areas in which programmed teaching has been effective. It concludes by discussing problems involved in comparing the effectiveness of programmed teaching with that of the conventional classroom teaching situation.

9. (a). The passage states: "Experimental psychologists typically do not take very seriously the evaluative experiments in which learning from programs is compared with learning from conventional teaching."

10. (e). The passage states: "The great strength of a program is that it permits the student to learn efficiently by himself."

11. (a). This is most clearly stated in the author's final paragraph, in which he calls for continued studies of programmed instruction even though some of the findings of comparative studies to date are of dubious value.

12. (d). The passage states: " . . . whereas one can describe fairly well the characteristics of a program, can one describe the characteristics of a classroom teaching situation so that the result of the comparison will have any generality? What kind of teacher is being compared to what kind of program?"

13. (e). The first sentence makes reference to bats, and the entire passage deals with flying.

14. (a). Rasselas says: "All skill ought to be exerted for universal good; every man has owed much to others, and ought to repay the kindness that he has received."

15. (d). The passage explicitly refers to the speaker as "the artist."

16. (c). The speaker is afraid that the wings will be put to malicious or dishonest use.

17. (c). Options (b), (d), and (e) are poetic forms and can thus be immediately disqualified. One might be inclined to select *fable* (a) on the basis of the "fabulous" nature of the artist's invention. The selection lacks, however, the concluding moral which is a necessary element of a fable. *Platonic dialogue* (c), therefore, is the best choice. In the selection, one speaker expresses a moral opinion and is questioned about his opinion by the other speaker.

18. (d). The artist states: "I will work only on this condition, that the art shall not be divulged, and that you shall not require me to make wings for any but ourselves."

19. (c). The writer regards the creation of art as a part of that process of "conceiving the universe" in which he enjoins the reader to participate. Earlier in the passage, he states that "music and poetry would resound along the streets" as a result of people learning to delight in the realities of the here and now.

20. (b). The writer states that children, "who play life, discern its true law and relations more clearly than men, who fail to live it worthily."

21. (a). This thought is expressed throughout the passage. It is, in fact, the writer's opening statement.

22. (e). The passage states: "Shams and delusions are esteemed for soundest truths, while reality is fabulous." This can be paraphrased as follows: nonexistent things are taken for realities, while realities are taken to be nonexistent.

23. (c). Once again, this is an idea that permeates the passage. It is summed up toward the end of the passage, where the writer states: "And we are enabled to apprehend at all what is sublime and noble only by the perpetual instilling and drenching of the reality that surrounds us."

24. (d). The passage deals with the nature of reality, our perception of it, and the role of God in the universe — issues which clearly fall into the domain of philosophy and theology.

18. Repertory Test

by Norman F. Watt

Pat: "How about a date?"

Robin: "No, thanks, I just ate."

A critical component of verbal ability is knowing the multiple meanings of many words. It is central to much of our humor and slang. Flexibility in dealing with the alternative meanings of words has long been regarded as part of overall vocabulary skill. Research during the last 15 years, however, has caused psychologists to view such vocabulary flexibility as especially important in the creative process and in personality development.

The skill that psychologists and educators place at the core of this flexibility is the ability to go beyond *functional fixedness*. An individual whose verbal skills rely on functional fixedness in vocabulary would give a word one primary meaning and always interpret that word in the same way, regardless of the context.

The Repertory Test, developed by the University of Denver psychologist Dr. Norman Watt, was designed to measure the ability to shift from one meaning of a given word to another, often subtler meaning. Dr. Watt based his test on homonyms, words that generally sound alike and also are spelled the same way, but have semantically distinguishable meanings. For example, *pool* of water and *pool* the game are homonyms.

INSTRUCTIONS

In the Repertory Test, you will be presented with a list of 24 simple words, each followed by 5 more words. You are to circle that word of the 5 which is closest in meaning to the first word given. For example:

RIGHT   head   wrong   loss   privilege   mountain

One meaning of the word right *is privilege, so you would circle* privilege *as the correct answer. Another example:*

HELP   pen   apple   servant   jump   full

One meaning of the word help *is servant or employee, so the word* servant *should be circled. In both of these examples, the correct answer is an unusual meaning of the word. You will find, in this vocabulary test, that the correct answer will often not be the first meaning that comes to mind.*

Give yourself three and a half minutes to complete the test. When your time is up, stop your work and turn the page to find your score.

1.	VICE	(fault)	book	fan	squad	band
2.	SOUND	craft	horn	term	ax	(water)
3.	CAST	(mold)	flow	fly	sail	pull
4.	HAIL	vessel	(shout)	taxi	pan	winter
5.	JUNK	hose	pail	file	(boat)	pet
6.	SCOPE	batter	court	(range)	port	pencil
7.	COMPACT	taps	hole	(agreement)	organ	spring
8.	BOARD	(meals)	song	capital	smoke	hunch
9.	TIE	salt	bank	verse	(clothing)	deck
10.	MATCH	earth	meter	opera	swallow	(firestick)
11.	KEY	drop	ring	ship	spirit	(pitch)
12.	TACK	tick	(approach)	matter	story	sand
13.	CHARM	(ornament)	scale	boy	seal	motor
14.	CHANGE	calf	diaper	cage	(switch)	deed
15.	CLUB	slip	(stick)	desire	host	draft
16.	LIST	toe	cup	(tilt)	people	side
17.	CELL	type	back	coin	poker	(unit)
18.	GRADE	(slope)	pan	see	duck	desk
19.	BARREL	roll	lot	(container)	grave	sage
20.	CORN	air	plaster	cap	(plants)	bullet
21.	LOCK	rail	(hair)	plum	bear	pit
22.	PLOT	season	wave	(section)	law	play
23.	STAGE	(table)	(carriage)	creed	actor	rifle
24.	BOND	dance	glass	base	(relation)	gate

SCORING

To score the test, compare your circled answers on the test to the Scoring Key below. Give yourself 1 point for each correct answer and write the total in the box below.

TOTAL
SCORE

SCORING KEY

1.	fault	13.	ornament
2.	water	14.	switch
3.	mold	15.	stick
4.	shout	16.	tilt
5.	boat	17.	unit
6.	range	18.	slope
7.	agreement	19.	container
8.	meals	20.	plants
9.	clothing	21.	hair
10.	firestick	22.	section
11.	pitch	23.	carriage
12.	approach	24.	relation

INTERPRETATION

Remember how much fun you had as a child discovering that a familiar word had a second and very different meaning? Not only were such experiences fun, they also served to broaden your vocabulary as you grew up. The Repertory Test can give you an indication of how well you can use your vocabulary to identify the subtle meanings of words when you are placed under the pressure of a time limit.

To do well on this test, you need to be able to combine a mental search for all meanings of the given word with the ability to think quickly and efficiently. A high score (18 to 24) suggests that you can work well in situations requiring rapid yet often subtle discriminations. This capacity is needed by translators, newspaper or magazine or book editors, police dispatchers, and air traffic controllers. Your score also indicates that you have the ability to shift from one conceptual set to another, a requirement of high-pressure occupations.

An average score on The Repertory Test (11 to 17) may provide you with more questions than answers about your ability. For example, how much did the time pressure affect your performance? Did you leap to the first alternative that seemed correct? Did you plod through, getting each item correct that you attempted but only getting partway through the test?

Each of these questions must be considered in your analysis of your score. An average performance on this test may not mean average vocabulary skills. Your score should be considered in light of your performances on the other verbal tests in *The Brain Game*.

A score of 10 or less suggests that this test was not much fun for you. And neither are many of the jokes that rely on the subtleties in language. Broadening your vocabulary through some structured practice could be very helpful. Just a few minutes each day spent browsing through a dictionary will increase your vocabulary. Word games and crossword puzzles can be both fun and educational for you. You will find that time spent increasing the range and depth of your verbal skills can be very rewarding.

19. Minnesota Vocabulary Test

In order to read a book intelligently, you've got to understand the words. In fact, having a good vocabulary is associated with high levels of many other verbal abilities. It's as though the words serve as building blocks for other specific intellectual abilities.

Such was the view in 1930 when University of Minnesota professor Dr. Melvin Haggerty and Stanford professor Dr. Alvin Eurich combined their efforts to produce the Minnesota Reading Examination (MRE). They wrote: "For a number of years a general college ability test had been administered to entering students. . . . It was thought desirable to devise several tests of more specific and special ability. Reading comprehension was considered of sufficient importance to success in college to justify the construction of a special test of this ability." The MRE was designed to meet what they saw as an immediate need in intellectual assessment.

One section of their examination is the Minnesota Vocabulary Test (MVT). The MVT will test your knowledge of *and* familiarity with words. You'll be forced to pull the words and their likely meanings from a different part of your memory than you would employ for words that you use every day. The MVT should serve as an interesting measure of the breadth of your vocabulary as well as your overall reading level.

INSTRUCTIONS

Before you begin the Minnesota Vocabulary Test, turn the page and remove the Answer Sheet. There are 100 words on the test, each followed by 4 words or phrases. You are to choose that word or phrase of the 4 that is the best definition of the first word, and mark your response on the Answer Sheet. For example:

author	(a) name	(b) originator	(c) reporter	(d) scholar
uncouth	(a) cruel	(b) bold	(c) uncultured	(d) robust

In the first example you should have marked (b), originator, as the best definition. In the next example the correct answer is (c), uncultured.

Give yourself six minutes in which to complete this test. You will need to work quickly. When your time is up, stop your work and turn the page to find your score.

1. surplus (a) an excess (b) coins (c) salaries (d) a surplice
2. affirm (a) to depict (b) to declare (c) to fix (d) to refuse
3. eternal (a) the beginning (b) the end (c) space (d) without end
4. restrain (a) to exhaust (b) to check (c) to exert (d) to reverse
5. silhouette (a) a cloth (b) a garment (c) a shadow (d) a streak
6. habitual (a) unusual (b) customary (c) irregular (d) to practice
7. immaculate (a) faulty (b) defiled (c) spotless (d) irrelevant
8. intimate (a) frightened (b) timid (c) familiar (d) to imitate
9. commemorate (a) to certify (b) to celebrate (c) noted (d) famous
10. retort (a) a charge (b) to speak back (c) civility (d) to control
11. sagacious (a) thoughtless (b) wise (c) old (d) sarcastic
12. casual (a) incidental (b) frequently (c) deathlike (d) costly
13. anonymous (a) synonymous (b) unacquainted (c) poisonous (d) nameless
14. mortal (a) a fragment (b) subject to death (c) dangerous (d) confounded
15. incredible (a) cruel (b) improbable (c) very small (d) unkind
16. legacy (a) a gift by will (b) to delegate (c) a loan (d) a legal procedure
17. ingenuity (a) cleverness (b) artifice (c) haste (d) novelty
18. stupor (a) stubborn (b) unyielding (c) lethargy (d) robust
19. indolent (a) weary (b) busy (c) lazy (d) thoughtless
20. mediocre (a) between (b) commonplace (c) extraordinary (d) meantime
21. feign (a) weak (b) to assume (c) to flinch (d) to invent
22. hypothesis (a) a supposition (b) a relation (c) a provision (d) proof
23. statute (a) a law (b) a piece of sculpture (c) a judgment (d) a book
24. cudgel (a) a club (b) to hide (c) to sneak (d) an injury
25. morass (a) an ocean (b) a moose (c) a swamp (d) a desert
26. luscious (a) bright (b) lucid (c) delicious (d) sour
27. gambol (a) to frolic (b) to gamble (c) to quarrel (d) noisy
28. credulous (a) to doubt (b) credible (c) positive (d) easily deceived
29. concise (a) sharp (b) to contract (c) brief (d) protracted
30. demote (a) to move away (b) remote (c) to reduce (d) to weaken
31. morose (a) pale (b) dark (c) ill humored (d) furious
32. odious (a) detestable (b) ill smelling (c) pleasant (d) peculiar
33. omniscient (a) universal (b) all knowing (c) infinite (d) ominous
34. cadence (a) sound (b) rhythm (c) slow (d) singing
35. subtle (a) wicked (b) stupid (c) crafty (d) beneath
36. unremitting (a) failure to pay (b) incessant (c) exacting (d) unpleasant
37. ruddy (a) robust (b) brawny (c) rough (d) reddish
38. nocturnal (a) poisonous (b) nightly (c) sentimental (d) underground
39. joust (a) to joke (b) a fight (c) to get rid of (d) to jump
40. precocious (a) dangerous (b) careful (c) bold (d) prematurely developed
41. reciprocate (a) to overcome (b) to avenge (c) to interchange (d) to mix
42. lore (a) song (b) learning (c) short stories (d) poetry
43. rancor (a) forbearance (b) a disease (c) malice (d) an animal
44. derisive (a) silly (b) scornful (c) troublesome (d) miserable
45. asunder (a) pulling (b) to tear (c) wide (d) apart
46. harbinger (a) forerunner (b) a message (c) a port (d) a bird
47. flaunt (a) to ignore (b) to discard (c) to display (d) to hide
48. querulous (a) inquisitive (b) complaining (c) noisy (d) agreeable
49. amenable (a) mean (b) docile (c) affectionate (d) related
50. interim (a) eternity (b) a period of time (c) time intervening (d) the beginning

ANSWER SHEET

19. Minnesota Vocabulary Test

	a b c d		a b c d		a b c d		a b c d
1.	0 0 0 0	26.	0 0 0 0	51.	0 0 0 0	76.	0 0 0 0
2.	0 0 0 0	27.	0 0 0 0	52.	0 0 0 0	77.	0 0 0 0
3.	0 0 0 0	28.	0 0 0 0	53.	0 0 0 0	78.	0 0 0 0
4.	0 0 0 0	29.	0 0 0 0	54.	0 0 0 0	79.	0 0 0 0
5.	0 0 0 0	30.	0 0 0 0	55.	0 0 0 0	80.	0 0 0 0
6.	0 0 0 0	31.	0 0 0 0	56.	0 0 0 0	81.	0 0 0 0
7.	0 0 0 0	32.	0 0 0 0	57.	0 0 0 0	82.	0 0 0 0
8.	0 0 0 0	33.	0 0 0 0	58.	0 0 0 0	83.	0 0 0 0
9.	0 0 0 0	34.	0 0 0 0	59.	0 0 0 0	84.	0 0 0 0
10.	0 0 0 0	35.	0 0 0 0	60.	0 0 0 0	85.	0 0 0 0
11.	0 0 0 0	36.	0 0 0 0	61.	0 0 0 0	86.	0 0 0 0
12.	0 0 0 0	37.	0 0 0 0	62.	0 0 0 0	87.	0 0 0 0
13.	0 0 0 0	38.	0 0 0 0	63.	0 0 0 0	88.	0 0 0 0
14.	0 0 0 0	39.	0 0 0 0	64.	0 0 0 0	89.	0 0 0 0
15.	0 0 0 0	40.	0 0 0 0	65.	0 0 0 0	90.	0 0 0 0
16.	0 0 0 0	41.	0 0 0 0	66.	0 0 0 0	91.	0 0 0 0
17.	0 0 0 0	42.	0 0 0 0	67.	0 0 0 0	92.	0 0 0 0
18.	0 0 0 0	43.	0 0 0 0	68.	0 0 0 0	93.	0 0 0 0
19.	0 0 0 0	44.	0 0 0 0	69.	0 0 0 0	94.	0 0 0 0
20.	0 0 0 0	45.	0 0 0 0	70.	0 0 0 0	95.	0 0 0 0
21.	0 0 0 0	46.	0 0 0 0	71.	0 0 0 0	96.	0 0 0 0
22.	0 0 0 0	47.	0 0 0 0	72.	0 0 0 0	97.	0 0 0 0
23.	0 0 0 0	48.	0 0 0 0	73.	0 0 0 0	98.	0 0 0 0
24.	0 0 0 0	49.	0 0 0 0	74.	0 0 0 0	99.	0 0 0 0
25.	0 0 0 0	50.	0 0 0 0	75.	0 0 0 0	100.	0 0 0 0

(Tear Out)

ANSWER SHEET

19. Minnesota Vocabulary Test

	a	b	c	d		a	b	c	d		a	b	c	d		a	b	c	d
1.	0	0	0	0	26.	0	0	0	0	51.	0	0	0	0	76.	0	0	0	0
2.	0	0	0	0	27.	0	0	0	0	52.	0	0	0	0	77.	0	0	0	0
3.	0	0	0	0	28.	0	0	0	0	53.	0	0	0	0	78.	0	0	0	0
4.	0	0	0	0	29.	0	0	0	0	54.	0	0	0	0	79.	0	0	0	0
5.	0	0	0	0	30.	0	0	0	0	55.	0	0	0	0	80.	0	0	0	0
6.	0	0	0	0	31.	0	0	0	0	56.	0	0	0	0	81.	0	0	0	0
7.	0	0	0	0	32.	0	0	0	0	57.	0	0	0	0	82.	0	0	0	0
8.	0	0	0	0	33.	0	0	0	0	58.	0	0	0	0	83.	0	0	0	0
9.	0	0	0	0	34.	0	0	0	0	59.	0	0	0	0	84.	0	0	0	0
10.	0	0	0	0	35.	0	0	0	0	60.	0	0	0	0	85.	0	0	0	0
11.	0	0	0	0	36.	0	0	0	0	61.	0	0	0	0	86.	0	0	0	0
12.	0	0	0	0	37.	0	0	0	0	62.	0	0	0	0	87.	0	0	0	0
13.	0	0	0	0	38.	0	0	0	0	63.	0	0	0	0	88.	0	0	0	0
14.	0	0	0	0	39.	0	0	0	0	64.	0	0	0	0	89.	0	0	0	0
15.	0	0	0	0	40.	0	0	0	0	65.	0	0	0	0	90.	0	0	0	0
16.	0	0	0	0	41.	0	0	0	0	66.	0	0	0	0	91.	0	0	0	0
17.	0	0	0	0	42.	0	0	0	0	67.	0	0	0	0	92.	0	0	0	0
18.	0	0	0	0	43.	0	0	0	0	68.	0	0	0	0	93.	0	0	0	0
19.	0	0	0	0	44.	0	0	0	0	69.	0	0	0	0	94.	0	0	0	0
20.	0	0	0	0	45.	0	0	0	0	70.	0	0	0	0	95.	0	0	0	0
21.	0	0	0	0	46.	0	0	0	0	71.	0	0	0	0	96.	0	0	0	0
22.	0	0	0	0	47.	0	0	0	0	72.	0	0	0	0	97.	0	0	0	0
23.	0	0	0	0	48.	0	0	0	0	73.	0	0	0	0	98.	0	0	0	0
24.	0	0	0	0	49.	0	0	0	0	74.	0	0	0	0	99.	0	0	0	0
25.	0	0	0	0	50.	0	0	0	0	75.	0	0	0	0	100.	0	0	0	0

(Tear Out)

51. finesse (a) the end (b) a veneer (c) delicate skill (d) fine
52. coercion (a) conspiracy (b) strategy (c) compulsion (d) attraction
53. furor (a) rage (b) noise (c) a quarrel (d) a flurry
54. comely (a) ugly (b) delicate (c) beautiful (d) weak
55. prolific (a) scarce (b) fruitful (c) reckless (d) profuse
56. trite (a) pointed (b) new (c) hackneyed (d) tried
57. collusion (a) combination (b) connivance (c) conflict (d) decision
58. implacable (a) to subdue (b) relieved (c) uncertain (d) unrelenting
59. delectable (a) eatable (b) expensive (c) delightful (d) fancy
60. facetious (a) friendly (b) morose (c) witty (d) stupid
61. fealty (a) fidelity (b) treason (c) humility (d) a tenant
62. unmitigated (a) unabated (b) undisturbed (c) relieved (d) unfinished
63. counterpart (a) the opposite (b) a duplicate (c) a part of a machine (d) a coverlet
64. cavalcade (a) a procession on horseback (b) a ceremony (c) a caravan (d) a sliding mass
65. austere (a) proud (b) stern (c) vain (d) cold
66. chalice (a) a cup (b) dew (c) a flower (d) vase
67. sumptuous (a) costly (b) abundant (c) credulous (d) cheap
68. addled (a) confused (b) added (c) poisoned (d) disgusted
69. gyration (a) a gypsy (b) gymnastics (c) rotation (d) vibration
70. enigma (a) a riddle (b) a contrivance (c) a taint (d) a brand
71. tacit (a) tactful (b) loud (c) implied (d) clever
72. salience (a) saline (b) projection (c) triviality (d) contempt
73. paradoxical (a) seemingly absurd (b) perfect (c) old-fashioned (d) metaphorical
74. surcease (a) consolation (b) sorrow (c) cessation (d) relief
75. phlegmatic (a) nervous (b) sluggish (c) happy (d) spasmodic
76. condiment (a) a relish (b) a dessert (c) vegetables (d) food
77. bizarre (a) a marketplace (b) peculiar (c) grotesque (d) imaginative
78. opulent (a) influential (b) wealthy (c) fleshy (d) lazy
79. premonitory (a) cliff (b) giving warning (c) of monetary value (d) hideous
80. bauble (a) a bubble (b) a showy plaything (c) idle talk (d) babble
81. cryptic (a) uncanny (b) elusive (c) hidden (d) pretentious
82. termagant (a) quarrelsome (b) an arctic bird (c) a geometric term (d) disorderly
83. panegyric (a) an assembly (b) a denunciation (c) an event (d) praise
84. omnivorous (a) all mighty (b) a carriage (c) all devouring (d) carnivorous
85. obsequious (a) obscure (b) yielding (c) secluded (d) aloof
86. nonchalance (a) a noise (b) an echo (c) indifference (d) perfunctory
87. cutlass (a) an ax (b) a knife (c) a sword (d) a spear
88. hiatus (a) an animal (b) a calamity (c) dread (d) a gap
89. perfunctory (a) fundamental (b) formal (c) mechanical (d) careful
90. harpy (a) a musical instrument (b) a fish (c) forerunner (d) a monster
91. gargoyle (a) oil (b) a medicine (c) projecting spout (d) a vulture
92. germane (a) German (b) contagious (c) relevant (d) different
93. specious (a) kind (b) roomy (c) plausible (d) special
94. animus (a) an animal (b) hatred (c) love (d) nameless
95. descried (a) described (b) scolded (c) discerned (d) denounced
96. orison (a) a bird (b) the East (c) prayer (d) a song
97. limpid (a) sea animal (b) transparent (c) lame (d) flimsy
98. anachronism (a) a wrong (b) a form of government (c) an incongruity (d) a creed
99. benison (a) kindness (b) flesh (c) a blessing (d) a prayer
100. genuflection (a) an inflection (b) a reflection (c) a bending of the knee (d) a review of the past

SCORING KEY

1. a	26. c	51. c	76. a
2. b	27. a	52. c	77. c
3. d	28. d	53. a	78. b
4. b	29. c	54. c	79. b
5. c	30. c	55. b	80. b
6. b	31. c	56. c	81. c
7. c	32. a	57. b	82. a
8. c	33. b	58. d	83. d
9. b	34. b	59. c	84. c
10. b	35. c	60. c	85. b
11. b	36. b	61. a	86. c
12. a	37. d	62. a	87. c
13. d	38. b	63. b	88. d
14. b	39. b	64. a	89. c
15. b	40. d	65. b	90. d
16. a	41. c	66. a	91. c
17. a	42. b	67. a	92. c
18. c	43. c	68. a	93. c
19. c	44. b	69. c	94. b
20. b	45. d	70. a	95. c
21. b	46. a	71. c	96. c
22. a	47. c	72. b	97. b
23. a	48. b	73. a	98. c
24. a	49. b	74. c	99. c
25. c	50. c	75. b	100. c

SCORING

To score the test, compare your responses on the Answer Sheet to the Scoring Key on the facing page. Give yourself 1 point for each correct answer and write the total score in the box below.

TOTAL
SCORE

TEST NORMS

RAW SCORE	PERCENTILE	RAW SCORE	PERCENTILE
93	99.96	46	80.28
92	99.88	45	78.65
91	99.81	44	76.76
90	99.73	43	74.61
89	99.69	42	72.47
88	99.67	41	70.32
87	99.66	40	68.17
86	99.64	39	65.89
85	99.63	38	63.46
84	99.60	37	61.04
83	99.57	36	58.62
82	99.54	35	56.20
81	99.51	34	53.60
80	99.48	33	50.83
79	99.37	32	48.06
78	99.19	31	45.29
77	99.01	30	42.51
76	98.83	29	39.65
75	98.64	28	36.69
74	98.50	27	33.74
73	98.39	26	30.78
72	98.28	25	27.83
71	98.18	24	25.16
70	98.07	23	22.79
69	97.89	22	20.41
68	97.64	21	18.04
67	97.37	20	15.66
66	97.11	19	13.53
65	96.85	18	11.64
64	96.56	17	9.75
63	96.24	16	7.86
62	95.92	15	5.97
61	95.60	14	4.56
60	95.28	13	3.63
59	94.77	12	2.70
58	94.05	11	1.78
57	93.33	10	.85
56	92.62	9	.35
55	91.90	8	.29
54	90.99	7	.23
53	89.88	6	.17
52	88.76	5	.11
51	87.65	4	.07
50	86.54	3	.05
49	85.18	2	.03
48	83.54	1	.01
47	81.91		

INTERPRETATION

In case you are wondering, yes, six minutes is the time limit that Professors Haggerty and Eurich set for the test in 1930. And it probably seemed too brief for the people taking it then, as well. The task, however, is intended to be a measure of how effectively you can search your memory and select the best definition from four choices. It is a measure of efficiency, and that means doing well under pressure.

Slow reading is often associated with a low vocabulary level. You can't read well if you are frequently blocked by difficult words. Those words may contain the essence of the author's reason for writing the paragraph, article, or chapter. Skipping them or puzzling over them works directly against achieving a high level of comprehension. That is the very reason that most reading programs spend time, initially, on enlarging students' vocabularies.

To make the interpretation of how you did on the MVT a bit more intriguing, we've included the norms from the original test manual. Find your score in the adjoining table and evaluate yourself in terms of how 5504 students performed on the test in 1928. This table shows that the average score for the MVT was about 33, falling at the 50th percentile. That is, a score of 33 is higher than the performance of 50 percent of the norm group; a score of 43 is about at the 75th percentile, or higher than 75 percent of the norm group; and so on.

A rough estimate of your ability level can be obtained by noting that two of three people taking the test score between 20 and 48. Thus if your score is near or above 48, you can feel confident that it represents a high level of vocabulary ability, and that you perform well under timed conditions. If you did not score well (or at least not as well as you would have liked), you may want to think about whether your performance indicates an insufficient vocabulary or difficulty under time pressure. Each requires you to take different steps to remedy the problem.

Zirchow VII
by Lyonel Feininger
The National Gallery of Art
Washington, D.C.

CHAPTER FOUR

THE HARDWARE

WHAT WE CALL THE HARDWARE OF THE MIND

is the brain's biological wiring of as many as 200 billion neurons. These neurons are tiny cells that are specialized for the integration and transmission of information. We are never really taught such hardware abilities as storing and retrieving memories, recognizing differences and similarities, and sorting and blocking extraneous data, but, at the appropriate time in our development, these abilities emerge. Our hardware and the way it functions can probably never be changed, although portions of it may develop differently depending on our circumstances. Nor do these functions arise from chance connections in the brain. The brain's circuitry — or hardware — is organically organized with great precision by an enormously complex, preprogrammed, genetically controlled system.

The hardware functions we are most concerned with here are memory and recognition. Memory functions can be classified into two types: *associative* and *nonassociative*. Associative memory can be compared to the index of a book. An index uses one idea as a key for releasing a large amount of related or associated data. The associative memory is a system that increases the efficiency of information acquisition, storage, and retrieval. If associative memory can be compared to the index of a book, then nonassociative memory is the central idea behind the book. Your nonassociative memory collects ideas through time. Similar ideas could be collected again and again, stored in different locations, and not necessarily associated with one another. In order to make connections between ideas and draw intelligent conclusions, the software or programming of your mind must come into play.

To carry the computer analogy one step futher, nonassociative memory can be said to be *location addressable*, because one must go to a particular location in the brain in order to find the specific information needed. Associative memory on the other hand is regarded as *content addressable*, because one can address particular categories of content with high-speed sequential processing.

The eight tests that follow will measure such hardware skills as memory functions, content and pattern recognition, and concentration. Most of the tests have very short time limits to help measure the speed and accuracy with which your brain can process and retrieve information. Incidentally, because millions of your brain's 200 billion neurons die every day, the younger test taker may have an advantage. On those tests measuring long-term memory skills, however, those who have been around longer may do better.

20. Matching Accuracy Test (Numbers)

Most office work in the 1930's consisted of what we today call paper-shuffling and was largely done by hand. Sensing a need for a way to evaluate how well a potential office worker could shuffle papers, the Psychological Corporation developed and published the Minnesota Vocational Test for Clerical Workers in 1933. The test's title was changed in 1946 to the Minnesota Clerical Test (MCT), though the test itself remained basically unchanged. As the manual for the MCT states: "Although it is old, the *Minnesota Clerical Test* enjoys widespread and successful use in business and industry and in schools. The nature of the test is such as to make its context timeless. The items are as appropriate today as they were in 1931 when the test was constructed."

The Matching Accuracy Test (MAT), which follows this introduction, is patterned after the MCT. Though the concept is similar, each section is half as long as its counterpart on the MCT.

The Matching Accuracy Test is in two parts. Test 20 measures how well and quickly you can compare sets of numbered pairs. Test 21 involves the ability to match pairs of names.

INSTRUCTIONS

In the test beginning below, you will be asked to compare 100 pairs of numbers. If the two numbers in a pair are exactly *the same, put a check mark (✔) on the line between them. If they are different, make no mark on the line. For example:*

8317421 ___✔___ 8317421
603142 _____ 603412

A check mark was made between the first pair because the numbers are exactly the same. The numbers in the second pair do not match.

Give yourself three and a half minutes to complete the test. Work as quickly as you can. When your time is up, stop your work and underline the last pair you have completed, then turn the page to score the test.

---

1.   347612 _____ ✓ _____ 347612
2.   960521498 _____ 960521478
3.   3726 ___ ✓ ___ 3726
4.   851079225 ___ ✓ ___ 851079225
5.   1438926 _____ 1438928
6.   2781 _____ 2791
7. 29560418347 ___ ✓ ___ 29560418347
8.   520 _____ 530
9.   3151684 ___ ✓ ___ 3151684
10.   65972 ___ ✓ ___ 65972

11. 465379826071 ___ ✓ ___ 465379826071
12. 25684137920 _____ 25684137929
13.   176 ___ ✓ ___ 176
14.   851964105 _____ 851964105
15.   52714386 _____ 53714386
16.   7285 ___ ✓ ___ 7285
17.   9451720863 _____ 9451720862
18. 358127649078 _____ 358127649978
19.   74216 ___ ✓ ___ 74216
20. 14705382973 _____ 14795382973

21.   2834 ___ ✓ ___ 2834
22. 291063647297 _____ 291063647299
23.   41625 _____ 41925
24.   782950443 ___ ✓ ___ 782950443
25.   68927 ___ ✓ ___ 68927
26.   521394849 _____ 521394848
27.   370651 ___ ✓ ___ 370651
28.   62539170 _____ 62537190
29.   4891627 _____ 4891629
30.   10423968 ___ ✓ ___ 10423968

31.   327 _____ 329
32. 382911876054 ___ ✓ ___ 382911876054
33.   3120449176 _____ 3120449976
34.   263587 _____ 263589
35. 89901742463 ___ ✓ ___ 89901742463
36.   6424 _____ 6426
37.   5820963 ___ ✓ ___ 5820963
38.   1724453019 _____ 1722453109
39.   817 ___ ✓ ___ 817
40. 52489076335 ___ ✓ ___ 52489076335

41.   717 _____ 719
42.   2985 _____ 2983
43.   778 _____ 798
44.   6039 ___ ✓ ___ 6039
45.   4901632 _____ 49091632
46.   312542 ___ ✓ ___ 312542
47.   59642 _____ 596642
48.   8973629 ___ ✓ ___ 8973629
49.   4139 _____ 4138
50.   63082 ___ ✓ ___ 63082

51.	79451026384	_____	79451036484
52.	324970165	___✓___	324970165
53.	18637	___✓___	18637
54.	2158462370	_____	2158463370
55.	554321	_____	554221
56.	521498072	_____	521498073
57.	697	___✓___	697
58.	370416553972	___✓___	370416553972
59.	3824	___✓___	3824
60	651243	___✓___	651243
61.	2437615	___✓___	2437615
62.	859032671403	___✓___	859032671403
63.	73611894	___✓___	73611894
64.	19254835760	___✓___	19254835760
65.	72483956	___✓___	72483956
66.	3647219231	_____	3647210231
67.	103642579683	_____	103642579883
68.	270	_____	279
69.	981076254	_____	981076354
70.	3829	___✓___	3829
71.	5607143	___✓___	5607143
72.	47132854694	_____	47132854994
73.	63843	_____	63842
74.	952187	___✓___	952187
75.	26974301	_____	26974311
76.	46203891	_____	46203871
77.	1829657743	___✓___	1829657743
78.	93427803569	_____	93427803566
79.	694271	___✓___	694271
80.	72019663	___✓___	72019663
81.	97861243750	_____	97861243750
82.	76948352	_____	76948352
83.	6250791	_____	6250991
84.	206985314757	_____	206985314757
85.	371093	_____	371093
86.	82516435	_____	82516435
87.	439	_____	439
88.	890561203574	_____	890561202574
89.	16929	_____	16930
90.	4793608512	_____	4793608512
91.	8205197	_____	8205197
92.	2369147510	_____	3269147510
93.	95206548	_____	95296548
94.	539274	_____	538274
95.	1463872954	_____	1463872954
96.	5039	_____	5030
97.	674930413825	_____	674930413825
98.	718	_____	718
99.	2430981526	_____	2430986526
100.	37289	_____	37289

#		#	
1.	✔	51.	
2.		52.	✔
3.	✔	53.	✔
4.	✔	54.	
5.		55.	
6.		56.	
7.	✔	57.	✔
8.	✔	58.	✔
9.	✔	59.	✔
10.	✔	60.	✔
11.	✔	61.	✔
12.		62.	✔
13.	✔	63.	✔
14.	✔	64.	✔
15.		65.	✔
16.	✔	66.	
17.		67.	
18.		68.	
19.	✔	69.	
20.		70.	✔
21.	✔	71.	✔
22.		72.	
23.		73.	
24.	✔	74.	✔
25.	✔	75.	
26.		76.	
27.	✔	77.	✔
28.		78.	
29.		79.	✔
30.	✔	80.	✔
31.		81.	✔
32.	✔	82.	✔
33.		83.	
34.		84.	✔
35.	✔	85.	✔
36.	✔	86.	✔
37.	✔	87.	✔
38.		88.	
39.	✔	89.	
40.	✔	90.	✔
41.		91.	✔
42.		92.	
43.		93.	
44.	✔	94.	
45.		95.	✔
46.	✔	96.	
47.	✔	97.	✔
48.	✔	98.	✔
49.		99.	
50.	✔	100.	✔

FOLD BACK TO SCORE

SCORING

To find your score, fold this page back on the dotted line and compare your answers to those on the Scoring Key. Give yourself 1 point for each correct answer. Do not count any of the questions that you did not complete. Write the total in the box below.

TOTAL SCORE

Now, go on to the Matching Accuracy Test (Names), which begins on the next page. At the end of that test will appear an Interpretation section for both of these tests.

21. Matching Accuracy Test (Names)

INSTRUCTIONS

In this test you will be asked to compare 100 pairs of fictitious names. If the two names in a pair are exactly the same, put a check mark (✔) on the line between them; if they are different, make no mark on the line. For example:

Hinkley Pinkly Co. _____ Hinkly Pinkly Co.
John R. Cardhill ___✔___ John R. Cardhill

A check mark was made between the second pair because the names are exactly the same. The names do not match in the first pair.

Give yourself four minutes to complete the test. Work as quickly as you can. When your time is up, stop your work and underline the last pair you have completed, then turn the page to score the test.

1.	B. Mauer & Green	_____	B. Maeur & Green
2.	Goodwin Cider Co.	✓	Goodwin Cider Co.
3.	Tex Gas Co.	✓	Tex Gas Co.
4.	Bill Mitchell & Son	_____	Bill Mitchel & Son
5.	Starling Marker Co.	✓	Starling Marker Co.
6.	Knudsen Bros.	✓	Knudsen Bros.
7.	A. R. Berry & Co.	_____	A. R. Berry Co.
8.	Hansen, T. L.	_____	Hanson, T. L.
9.	Bragg & Son	_____	Bragg & Sons
10.	Kenneth Dalton	✓	Kenneth Dalton
11.	J. Dunn & Sons	_____	J. Dunn & Son
12.	Glass & Magnam	_____	Glass & Magnum
13.	S. Z. Cicerelli	_____	S. Z. Cicirelli
14.	Joel Bardsley	✓	Joel Bardsley
15.	R. L. Woodsworth	_____	R. L. Woodworth
16.	*Centennial Revue*	✓	*Centennial Revue*
17.	Paulette Ternier	_____	Paulete Ternier
18.	Jarpo Shop	_____	Jarpo's Shop
19.	Heyer Co.	_____	Heyer, Inc.
20.	Lonne Drew	_____	Lonne & Drew
21.	Hippo Trampolene Co.	_____	Hippo Trampline Co.
22.	Lieger & Kirsche	_____	Leiger & Kirsche
23.	B. J. Manis	✓	B. J. Manis
24.	Tolle Lbr. Co.	_____	Toll Lbr. Co.
25.	Parker's	✓	Parker's
26.	Belle Koff	_____	Bell Koff
27.	Stanley Bag Co.	✓	Stanley Bag Co.
28.	Wilson & Gander	_____	Wilsen & Gander
29.	Marhnson's	✓	Marhnson's
30.	Canopy Panoply Co.	✓	Canopy Panoply Co.
31.	Lesley Wallboard Co.	✓	Lesley Wallboard Co.
32.	Converse Rodeo	✓	Converse Rodeo
33.	Norton Rock Co.	_____	Norten Rock Co.
34.	G. G. Ferguson	✓	G. G. Ferguson
35.	Feister Courier	✓	Fiester Courier
36.	B. F. Grunion	✓	B. F. Grunion
37.	Nexus, Tod	_____	Nexus, Tad
38.	Christopher Iron Co.	✓	Christopher Iron Co.
39.	D. F. Rappaport	✓	D. F. Rappaport
40.	Ruth Iakley	_____	Ruth B. Oakley
41.	Gaine, Inc.	✓	Gaine, Inc.
42.	R. J. Killingworth	_____	R. J. Killinworth
43.	Allison Barrett	_____	Allison Barret
44.	Chippendale	_____	Clippendale
45.	B.U.Y. Motor Co.	_____	B.U.Y. Moter Co.
46.	Marten & Co.	_____	Martin & Co.
47.	T. Wein & Co.	✓	T. Wien & Co.
48.	Comm & Co.	✓	Comm & Co.
49.	Footstep Shoe Co.	✓	Footstep Shoe Co.
50.	Walford Lbr. Co.	_____	Walferd Lbr. Co.

51. Brazilian National_____Barzilian Nat'l
52. Extron Corp.___✓___Extron Corp.
53. Radiant Mfg. Co._____Radant Mfg. Co.
54. I. Garrick___✓___I. Garrick
55. M. Nichols Co._____N. Nichols Co.
56. Baumann, P. K._____Bauman, P. K.
57. Costley, R.E.___✓___Costley, R. E.
58. Harold, K. A.___✓___Harold, K. A.
59. Soldo, Inc._____Soldo Co.
60. Oyes Mfg. Co.___✓___Oyes Mfg. Co.

61. Alois Diane Lemand_____Alois Dianne Lemand
62. Richard Dougherty_____Richard I. Dougherty
63. Russell Record Co.___✓___Russell Record Co.
64. Ralph Reagan_____Ralph Reagen
65. Johnson's Deli___✓___Johnson's Deli
66. Eunice E. Wemme_____Eunice E. Weme
67. Sarah Richelle___✓___Sarah Richelle
68. Vargo Drywall Co._____Cargo Drywall & Co.
69. Borous & Bro._____Borus & Bro.
70. Birdstar, P. D._____Birdster, P. D.

71. Rechter, G. E._____Richter, G. E.
72. V. M. Pattresen___✓___V. M. Pattresen
73. Pureem Gas Co.___✓___Pureem Gas Co.
74. Mericott Co.___✓___Mericott Co.
75. Indianapolis Mfg. Co.___✓___Inidanapolis Mfg. Co.
76. Donnely, J. S._____Donneley, J. S.
77. Bensen & Co._____Benson & Co.
78. Neulmann, C. S.___✓___Neulmann, C. S.
79. Anderson & Co.___✓___Anderson & Co.
80. Valporan, D. H.___✓___Valporan, D. H.

81. Lavers Bros.___✓___Lavers Bros.
82. Lemens Gloves Co._____Lemens Glove Co.
83. Action Print Co.___✓___Action Print Co.
84. Brahme Co._____Brahne Co.
85. J. A. Harris___✓___J. A. Harris
86. Zinda & Co.___✓___Zinda & Co.
87. Grace Harmon_____Grace Harmen
88. Case Duplicating Co.___✓___Case Duplicating Co.
89. Haste Box Co.___✓___Haste Box Co.
90. Benedict Co._____Benedict & Co.

91. Larry Speer & Co._____Larry Speer Co.
92. Cornwall Day_____Cornwell Day
93. L.F.R. Knudsen & Sons___✓___L.F.R. Knudsen & Sons
94. Western Nat'l Bank___✓___Western Nat'l Bank
95. Dorcas, Ltd.___✓___Dorcas, Ltd.
96. M. Steiner_____M. Stiener
97. Masqueres_____Masqueris
98. Pendleton Mills___✓___Pendleton Mills
99. Greeley Institute_____Greeley's Institute
100. Bill Tepper___✓___Bill Tepper

1.		51.	
2.	✔	52.	✔
3.	✔	53.	
4.	✔	54.	✔
5.	✔	55.	
6.	✔	56.	
7.		57.	✔
8.		58.	✔
9.		59.	
10.	✔	60.	✔
11.		61.	
12.		62.	
13.		63.	✔
14.	✔	64.	
15.		65.	✔
16.	✔	66.	
17.		67.	✔
18.		68.	
19.		69.	
20.		70.	
21.		71.	
22.		72.	✔
23.	✔	73.	✔
24.		74.	✔
25.	✔	75.	
26.		76.	
27.	✔	77.	
28.	✔	78.	✔
29.	✔	79.	✔
30.	✔	80.	✔
31.	✔	81.	✔
32.	✔	82.	
33.		83.	✔
34.	✔	84.	
35.		85.	✔
36.	✔	86.	✔
37.		87.	
38.	✔	88.	✔
39.	✔	89.	✔
40.		90.	
41.	✔	91.	
42.		92.	
43.		93.	✔
44.		94.	✔
45.		95.	✔
46.		96.	
47.		97.	
48.	✔	98.	✔
49.	✔	99.	
50.		100.	✔

FOLD BACK TO SCORE

SCORING

To find your score, fold this page back on the dotted line and compare your answers to those on the Scoring Key. Give yourself 1 point for each correct answer. Do not count any of the questions that you did not complete. Write your total on both tests (numbers and names) in the boxes below.

TOTAL SCORE: NUMBERS (20) ☐

TOTAL SCORE: NAMES (21) ☐

INTERPRETATION

Given enough time, you would score 100 percent on each part of the MAT. But you probably did not have enough time to study each pair. Your task was to answer quickly and work out a trade-off for yourself between speed and accuracy. The trade-off is similar to the problems in judging a typist. Whose work is "better," the person who can type 120 words per minute with four errors or someone who works at 60 words per minute with zero errors? Your answer would probably be "It depends." It does depend, on the relative importance of speed and accuracy for a particular project.

When the MCT was originally developed, employers used it to find out how fast someone could accurately perform clerical tasks; thus the test became associated with secretarial and clerical positions where speed was of the essence. Today, however, the same skills are no longer strictly clerical in nature. In fact the need for this ability in clerical tasks has decreased. Now a word processor can even correct errors in your spelling, using words programmed into its memory. Computers handle routine calculations as fast as we can hit the start key.

For the 1980's and beyond, the skills measured by the MAT are required in many technical situations. Quality-control professionals in companies producing pharmaceuticals or computer chips must make immediate and accurate checks on products. Computer data inputting and manuscript proofreading demand the matching skill measured by these tests.

The norms for the MAT are as follows:

PERFORMANCE LEVEL	NUMBERS	NAMES
Strong	65-100	65-100
Average	52-64	50-64
Weak	0-51	0-49

Remember as you interpret your own score that the MAT is a test measuring accuracy in a high-speed situation. One sneeze could have cost you several points. And some people find they score lower than they would like because they can't avoid reading the names in the second part of the test. To do well you must treat each letter as just that, one letter filling a space to be compared to another letter in a corresponding space.

It's interesting to note that research shows women usually outperform men on this type of test. Though science does not yet understand the neurophysiological reasons for this difference, it does appear that the woman's brain is more thoroughly equipped for performing accurately under time pressure.

22. Recall-of-Observations Test

We observe things every day that we scarcely notice. All of what we see is stored somewhere in our memories, but how accessible is this information? Is it only the "important" information that makes it through to the conscious mind?

Some psychologists have found that the ability to recall observations is highly correlated with overall intelligence, and that remembering such information relies on specific memory abilities. The test that follows this one, Test 23, will also test your ability to remember, but it will use a multiple choice format rather than the recall process needed to do well on this one.

Memory research proves that recognizing a correct answer among several choices is an easier task than trying to recall that same answer without any visual clues whatsoever. The Recall-of-Observations Test is designed to measure the *recall* process in order to assess how much information people retain about the world around them.

Because of the rush of incoming stimuli, the brain filters out much of what is repetitious or irrelevant. Yet who is to say what will become important? To a truly observant mind — like that of a scientist or detective — even the most insignificant data may turn out to be vital.

INSTRUCTIONS

In the Recall-of-Observations Test, you will be presented with 32 questions about familiar objects. Your task is to visualize the object and then answer the question. Use the spaces provided to record your responses. This test is untimed.

1. It is a clear, starry night, and you see a crescent moon in the sky that looks like the drawing in Figure A. Is the moon *waxing* or *waning*? That is, if you were to return tomorrow night, would you find the moon fuller or less full, brighter or darker?

2. On a standard traffic light, is the green on *top* or *bottom*?

3. The stripes of a man's tie usually slant down in what direction (*left* or *right*) from the wearer's view?

4. In the Lincoln Memorial, which foot on the statue of Lincoln is in front?

5. In Grant Wood's painting *American Gothic,* is the man to the viewer's *left* or *right*?

6. In which hand is the Statue of Liberty's torch?

7. Name the five colors on a Campbell's soup label.

8. What two letters of the alphabet do not appear on a telephone dial?

9. What two digits on a telephone dial are not accompanied by letters?

10. When you walk, do your arms swing *with* or *against* the rhythm of you legs?

11. How many matches are in a standard pack?

12. On the American flag, is the uppermost stripe *red* or *white*?

13. What is the lowest number on an FM radio dial?

14. On a standard typewriter, over which number is the "%" symbol?

15. Which way does the red diagonal slash go in the international "no parking" or "no smoking" sign, *upper left to lower right* or *lower left to upper right*?

16. How many channels are there on a standard VHF television dial? (Careful, now.)

17. Which side of a woman's blouse has the buttonholes?

18. Do books have their even-numbered pages on the *left* or *right*?

19. In Figure B there are two dice. One has the pips arranged in the standard way, as you have seen them on virtually every die you have ever handled. The other is a mirror image, with the pips oriented backward. Which is the "real" die, the one on the *left* or the *right*?

20. On which side of a sink is the cold water faucet?

21. How many sides are there on a standard pencil?

22. Sleepy, Happy, Sneezy, Grumpy, Dopey, and Doc. Name the seventh dwarf.

23. How many hot dogs are in a standard package?

24. How many hot-dog buns are in a standard package?

25. In which direction does the lettering run on a standard pencil (*eraser to tip* or *tip to eraser*)?

26. On which card in the deck is the card maker's trademark?

27. On which side of a venetian blind is the cord that adjusts the opening between the slats?

28. On the back of a $5 bill is the Lincoln Memorial. What's in the center on the back side of a $1 bill?

29. There are 12 buttons on a Touch-Tone telephone. What symbols are on the two buttons that bear no digits?

30. The names of what things are "hidden" on the back of a $5 bill?

31.-32. There are two one-eyed jacks in a typical deck (Figure C). Which suit faces right?

32. Which suit faces left?

1. _____WAXING_____X____

2. _____BOTTOM_____-____

3. _____LEFT_____

4. _____RIGHT_____

5. _____RIGHT_____

6. _____LEFT_____X_____

7. _GOLD____RED____WHITE_____
   BLACK and _BLUE_____

8. _____Q___ and ___X_____

9. _____1___ and ___0_____

10. ____AGAINST_____

11. ____TWENTY_____

12. ____RED_____

13. _____88_____

14. _____9___·__Y_____

15. _UL_TO_LR_____

16. _____13_____X_____

17. ____RIGHT_____

18. ____LEFT_____

19. ____RIGHT_____

20. ____RIGHT_____

21. ____SIXIL_____

22. ___KASHEVL_____

23. _____10_____

24. ____TIP_8_____

25. _TIP_TO_ERASER_____

26. _ACE_/SPADES_____

27. __RIGHT_OR___X_____

28. JEFFERSON_MEMORIAL_X_____

29. ____#___ and ___✳_____

30. ____STATES_____

31. ____HEARTS____X_____

32. __DIAMONDS___X_____

Figure A.

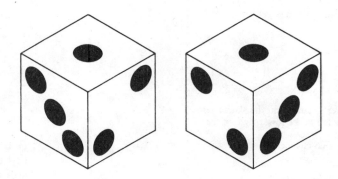

Figure B.

Figure C.

1. The crescent moon is waning. Tomorrow night it will be darker. To keep it all straight, remember DOC. When the crescent's arms point to the left and the moon has a curve like that on a capital letter D, the moon is waxing, or getting fuller. When the crescent has a curve like a capital C, as in the illustration, the moon is on the wane. First comes the D curve, then the full moon, then the C curve: DOC.
2. Bottom
3. Left
4. Right foot
5. Right
6. Right hand
7. Black, white, red, gold, and yellow
8. Q and Z
9. 1 and 0
10. Against
11. Twenty
12. Red
13. 88 (megahertz)
14. "5"
15. From the viewer's standpoint, the slash goes from the upper left to the lower right of the circle.
16. Twelve (there is no channel 1)
17. Right
18. Left
19. The real die is on the right.
20. Right
21. Six
22. Bashful
23. Hot dogs come in packages of ten.
24. Hot-dog rolls come in packets of eight. Naturally.
25. The writing on a pencil runs from tip to eraser, a result of the right-handedness of our species and the desire of pencil manufacturers to have their logos read by the widest audience.
26. The ace of spades.
27. Generally, the slat-adjustment cord is on the left.
28. The word "ONE"
29. * and #. The Bell System uses these symbols for custom-calling features.
30. You may need a magnifying glass to see them, but the names of 26 states can be found on the back of a $5 bill. Above the columns on the Lincoln Memorial, between the decorative figures that are directly above each column, are the names of 11 states — Delaware, Pennsylvania, New Jersey, Georgia, Connecticut, Massachusetts, Maryland, Carolina (sic), Hampshire (sic), Virginia, and New York. Fifteen more states appear, in even smaller type, on the top tier of the monument.
31. The jack of spades faces right.
32. The jack of hearts faces left.

FOLD BACK TO SCORE

SCORING

To find your score, fold this page back on the dotted line and compare your answers to those on the Scoring Key. Give yourself 1 point for each correct answer. You must answer the entire question correctly to score a point. There are 32 points possible. Add up your total and write it in the box below.

TOTAL
SCORE

INTERPRETATION

A high score on the Recall-of-Observations Test (29 or above) earns you accolades for both your ability of recall in general and your high level of observational skills. Your score suggests that you have an effective remembering process and are able to pull relatively insignificant items from your long term memory.

A score of 26 to 28 is considered very good. You have apparently paid close attention to objects and events as they came your way. This level of observational skill is very useful in occupations such as medicine, research, and the sciences.

If you scored from 17 to 25, your ability to recall observations falls into the average range. Although the skills tested by the Recall-of-Observations Test may not appear important to you at first glance, the ability to recall bits of information from memory can be important to career advancement as well as to basic survival.

If you scored low on the test (16 or below), you need to do some serious thinking about whether your score represents a lack of memory ability, a lack of attention toward things around you, or a combination of the two. You may wish to improve your memory ability by consciously observing objects and events and practicing memorization. Also keep in mind that in a test like this, age can be a factor. Younger people have greater memory skills, so you will need to take this into consideration when analyzing your score.

23. Memory Recognition Test

by James H. Johnson and Daniel Klinger

Even if you haven't seen someone you know for a very long time, you can usually pick that person out of a group. You can recognize his or her features although you may not be able to describe those features from memory. A similar phenomenon occurs in memory when you are presented with a question and a list of answers and then asked to pick the correct alternative. You unconsciously scan your memory for signals to indicate which choices are incorrect as you simultaneously scan for information about which single choice is correct.

The memory process involved in such tasks is termed *recognition*. Psychologists generally view recognition as an easier and more efficient process than recall, in which there are no alternatives to choose from. In recognition, each choice presented stimulates a different part of the information stored in memory. You can then compare that retrieved information to the question and determine which alternative is correct.

In 1976, the University of Utah professors James Johnson and Daniel Klinger decided to use the recognition format to examine the differences in memory processes among groups of schizophrenic patients, neurotic individuals, and "no mental illness" subjects. In order to design a test that could be used across the United States, Drs. Johnson and Klinger reviewed national newsmagazines published over the previous 30 years. They selected 25 facts and events, and wrote a multiple choice question based on each one. The resulting test, which follows, was then used to examine memory differences among the groups involved.

INSTRUCTIONS

In the Memory Recognition Test, you will be presented with 25 questions, each with multiple-choice answers. Use the Answer Sheet that follows to record your responses.

There is no time limit on the test. Answer as many questions as you can, then turn the page to find your score.

---

1. Who was convicted of killing eight nurses in Chicago in 1966?
   (a) Miranda
   (b) no one; no suspect was ever found
   (c) Speck
   (d) no one; suspect was acquitted
   (e) Starkweather
   (f) DeSalvo

2. What is the name of Harry Truman's daughter?
   (a) Mildred
   (b) Margaret
   (c) Linda
   (d) Mamie
   (e) Bess
   (f) Julie

3. What was the name of the U-2 pilot shot down over Russia?
   (a) Porter
   (b) Rickenbacker
   (c) Hall
   (d) Mitchell
   (e) Howard
   (f) Powers

4. What happened to astronauts Grissom, White, and Chaffee?
   (a) became mentally ill after flight
   (b) landed on moon
   (c) had trouble returning from orbit
   (d) met untimely deaths
   (e) were divorced
   (f) smuggled stamps aboard capsule

5. For what dance is the Peppermint Lounge famous?
   (a) twist
   (b) monster mash
   (c) jitterbug
   (d) peppermint mash
   (e) frug
   (f) bunny hop

6. What is SAC?
   (a) Omaha-based squadron
   (b) dance
   (c) dress
   (d) gangland killing
   (e) Strategic Air Command
   (f) waterbed

7. What was the "foaming cleanser?"
   (a) Brillo
   (b) Comet
   (c) Bab-O
   (d) Tuffy
   (e) Ajax
   (f) Drano

8. As what did Alexander Dubček become famous?
   (a) Notre Dame All-American
   (b) Czechoslovakian leader
   (c) concert pianist
   (d) New York Yankee shortstop
   (e) Hungarian premier
   (f) ballet dancer

9. Who was convicted of shooting George Wallace?
   (a) Carmichael
   (b) Brennan
   (c) Clay
   (d) Carver
   (e) Bremer
   (f) Seale

10. Who was Mary Jo Kopechne?
    (a) student killed at Kent State
    (b) woman who died on Chappaquiddick Island
    (c) secretary who transcribed Watergate tapes
    (d) fugitive Weatherman
    (e) Symbionese Liberation Army member
    (f) Olympic gold medal winner

11. Charles Manson was convicted of killing what famous person?
    (a) Chambers
    (b) Mansfield
    (c) Crane
    (d) Garland
    (e) Tate
    (f) Polanski

12. Who played Davy Crockett?
    (a) Fess Parker
    (b) Clint Walker
    (c) Buddy Ebsen
    (d) James Arness
    (e) Guy Williams
    (f) Dennis Weaver

13. Who was convicted of killing Robert Kennedy?
    (a) Oswald
    (b) Ruby
    (c) Sirhan
    (d) Brown
    (e) Mohajer
    (f) Ray

ANSWER SHEET

23. Memory Recognition Test

	a	b	c	d	e	f			a	b	c	d	e	f
1.	0	0	0	0	0	0		14.	0	0	0	0	0	0
2.	0	0	0	0	0	0		15.	0	0	0	0	0	0
3.	0	0	0	0	0	0		16.	0	0	0	0	0	0
4.	0	0	0	0	0	0		17.	0	0	0	0	0	0
5.	0	0	0	0	0	0		18.	0	0	0	0	0	0
6.	0	0	0	0	0	0		19.	0	0	0	0	0	0
7.	0	0	0	0	0	0		20.	0	0	0	0	0	0
8.	0	0	0	0	0	0		21.	0	0	0	0	0	0
9.	0	0	0	0	0	0		22.	0	0	0	0	0	0
10.	0	0	0	0	0	0		23.	0	0	0	0	0	0
11.	0	0	0	0	0	0		24.	0	0	0	0	0	0
12.	0	0	0	0	0	0		25.	0	0	0	0	0	0
13.	0	0	0	0	0	0								

ANSWER SHEET

23. Memory Recognition Test

	a	b	c	d	e	f			a	b	c	d	e	f
1.	0	0	0	0	0	0		14.	0	0	0	0	0	0
2.	0	0	0	0	0	0		15.	0	0	0	0	0	0
3.	0	0	0	0	0	0		16.	0	0	0	0	0	0
4.	0	0	0	0	0	0		17.	0	0	0	0	0	0
5.	0	0	0	0	0	0		18.	0	0	0	0	0	0
6.	0	0	0	0	0	0		19.	0	0	0	0	0	0
7.	0	0	0	0	0	0		20.	0	0	0	0	0	0
8.	0	0	0	0	0	0		21.	0	0	0	0	0	0
9.	0	0	0	0	0	0		22.	0	0	0	0	0	0
10.	0	0	0	0	0	0		23.	0	0	0	0	0	0
11.	0	0	0	0	0	0		24.	0	0	0	0	0	0
12.	0	0	0	0	0	0		25.	0	0	0	0	0	0
13.	0	0	0	0	0	0								

14. Don Knotts is most famous for playing what character on television?
    (a) Gomer Pyle
    (b) Barney Fife
    (c) Mr. Figg
    (d) Agent 008
    (e) Mr. Peepers
    (f) Pinky Lee

15. Lloyd Bucher commanded what vessel?
    (a) *Nautilus*
    (b) *Missouri*
    (c) *Thresher*
    (d) *Triton*
    (e) *Monterey*
    (f) *Pueblo*

16. What was the name of the television series that starred Robert Stack and was set during Prohibition?
    (a) *Eliot Ness*
    (b) *Dillinger*
    (c) *Gang Busters*
    (d) *The FBI*
    (e) *The Untouchables*
    (f) *The Roaring Twenties*

17. Which doctor performed the first transplant operation?
    (a) Barnard
    (b) Christianson
    (c) Shumway
    (d) De Bakey
    (e) Salk
    (f) Schumberg

18. How did Clay Shaw become known?
    (a) through Supreme Court
    (b) through Jim Garrison
    (c) through Cassius Clay
    (d) through Andy Granatelli
    (e) through Texas politics
    (f) through Watergate

19. Name a nonpolitician involved in the Profumo scandal.
    (a) Nancy Rice
    (b) Steven Ward
    (c) Walter Jenkins
    (d) Ruby Keeler
    (e) Billy Sol Estes
    (f) Robert Vesco

20. Who wrote a false autobiography of Howard Hughes?
    (a) Parrish
    (b) Brooks
    (c) Updike
    (d) Irving
    (e) Roth
    (f) Getty

21. What was the name of Ozzie and Harriet's oldest son?
    (a) Dick
    (b) Rick
    (c) Eddie
    (d) David
    (e) Bob
    (f) Wally

22. In what state is the Attica prison?
    (a) Maryland
    (b) New Jersey
    (c) Alabama
    (d) California
    (e) New York
    (f) Ohio

23. Who was *Cosmopolitan* magazine's first male centerfold?
    (a) Joe Namath
    (b) Burt Reynolds
    (c) Robert Redford
    (d) Henry Kissinger
    (e) Paul Newman
    (f) Jack Bradford

24. Who was convicted of killing Martin Luther King, Jr.?
    (a) Harvey
    (b) Connor
    (c) Meredith
    (d) Muhammad
    (e) Schenely
    (f) Ray

25. Who was George McGovern's first running mate in the 1972 presidential election?
    (a) Miller
    (b) Shriver
    (c) Eagleton
    (d) Humphrey
    (e) Allison
    (f) Hart

SCORING

To score the test, compare your responses on the Answer Sheet to those on the Scoring Key below. Give yourself 1 point for each correct answer and write the total in the box below.

TOTAL SCORE

SCORING KEY

1. c	14. b
2. b	15. f
3. f	16. e
4. d	17. a
5. a	18. b
6. e	19. b
7. e	20. d
8. b	21. d
9. e	22. e
10. b	23. b
11. e	24. f
12. a	25. c
13. c	

INTERPRETATION

First, let us mention that Drs. Johnson and Klinger found no differences among their schizophrenic, neurotic, and "no mental illness" subjects when it came to recognition. So no matter how you scored, your performance won't serve as an emotional diagnostic tool.

The Memory Recognition Test (MRT) does measure your ability to scan your memory for information relevant to the questions and relevant to the incorrect alternatives. A high score (19 to 25) may certainly indicate that you were well read and informed about public events during the years covered by the MRT. On the other hand, you may have selected the correct answers by unconsciously letting each alternative stimulate your memory and then simply seeing if the output matched the question.

If you scored in the average range (11 to 18), think about the memory techniques you used during the test. If you treated it as a recall test rather than one using recognition, you made the test more difficult than necessary and your score may have suffered in the process. Let the incorrect alternatives help you whenever you are faced with a multiple-choice recognition test.

If you are very young, a low score on the MRT (0 to 10) would be understandable. Since the items were selected from national newsmagazines published from 1946 to 1976, many of the events may have taken place before your time. Unless you are a trivia buff, a low score could represent a lack of experience rather than a low amount of information stored in your memory.

If these reasons do not fit your situation, a low score may suggest a lack of interest on your part about what is going on in the world. Scoring higher on a test such as the MRT does not require that you become smarter but that you expend the energy needed to learn about the events going on around you.

EXPLANATORY ANSWERS

1. (c). In 1967 Richard Speck was found guilty of the July 1966 stabbing and strangulation murders of eight student nurses.

2. (b). Mary Margaret Truman was the only child of Bess Wallace and Harry Truman and the first female only child of a President to occupy the White House.

3. (f). Francis Gary Powers was shot down over the Soviet Union on May 1, 1960.

4. (d). Virgil "Gus" Grissom, Edward White, and Roger Chaffee were killed when a fire occurred inside Apollo I while the craft was still on the launching pad, on January 27, 1967.

5. (a). Then located in the Knickerbocker Hotel in New York City, the Peppermint Lounge nightclub gave the twist its start.

6. (e). The United States Air Force's Strategic Air Command, SAC, is a force prepared to deliver an atom bomb over an enemy target, which serves as a deterrent to Russian attack.

7. (e). "Use Ajax, the foaming cleanser — floats the dirt right down the drain."

8. (b). Soviet-educated Alexander Dubček's term as first secretary of the Communist Party of Czechoslovakia (1968-1969) saw the Soviet occupation of Czechoslovakia and the termination of Dubček's liberal political program.

9. (e). Arthur Herman Bremer, a 21-year-old Milwaukeean, shot George C. Wallace and three others on May 15, 1972, in Maryland; Wallace's injuries resulted in permanent paralysis from the hips down.

10. (b). Mary Jo Kopechne, a 28-year-old New Jersey woman and former member of Robert F. Kennedy's staff, died when a car driven by Senator Edward M. Kennedy plunged off a small wooden bridge on Chappaquiddick Island in Massachusetts on July 18, 1969.

11. (e). During the longest criminal trial in California history, Charles Manson and three female "family" members were convicted of slaying actress Sharon Tate, wife of film director Roman Polanski, and six others in August 1969.

12. (a). Fess Parker played Davy in a Walt Disney three-part television movie in 1954-1955.

13. (c). A 24-year-old Jordanian nationalist, Sirhan Bishara Sirhan, shot Robert F. Kennedy and wounded five others following the California presidential primary, on June 5, 1968; Kennedy, with bullets lodged in his brain and neck, died 25 hours later.

14. (b). Don Knotts costarred as Deputy Sheriff Barney Fife with Andy Griffith in the CBS series *The Andy Griffith Show*, which debuted in 1960.

15. (f). The electronic surveillance ship *U.S.S. Pueblo*, commanded by Lloyd Bucher, was captured by North Korea on January 23, 1968.

16. (e). *The Untouchables* (1959-1963) starred Robert Stack as Eliot Ness, leader of a group of crime fighters from the U.S. Treasury Department.

17. (a). Dr. Christiaan Barnard performed the first successful heart transplant, in Cape Town, South Africa, on December 3, 1967; the patient, Louis Washkanski, lived for 18 days.

18. (b). On February 27, 1970, Clay L. Shaw filed a $5-million lawsuit against New Orleans District Attorney Jim Garrison for his involvement in the prosecution of Shaw on charges of conspiring to assassinate President John F. Kennedy; Shaw was acquitted of those charges in March 1969.

19. (b). Osteopath Stephen Ward lent his apartment for the infamous rendezvous of British War Secretary John Profumo and model Christine Keeler in that 1963 sex scandal.

20. (d). Clifford Irving and his wife Edith were convicted on June 16, 1972, of writing the "autobiography" refuted as "totally fantastic fiction" by Howard Hughes.

21. (d). On one of America's favorite radio and TV shows, Ozzie and Harriet had two sons, David, the oldest, and Ricky.

22. (e). The Attica prison, the scene in 1971 of bloody riots, is located in New York State.

23. (b). Burt Reynolds posed free as the nude centerfold in *Cosmo*'s April 1972 issue.

24. (f). James Earl Ray, convicted of assassinating Dr. Martin Luther King, Jr., in Memphis, Tennessee, on April 4, 1968, was arrested in London on June 8 after the most extensive manhunt in police history.

25. (c). McGovern's handling of the nomination for Vice-President and dropping from the ticket of Missouri Senator Thomas Eagleton in 1972 is considered to have been a major reason for his overwhelming defeat.

24. Figure Recognition Test

by S. A. Karp

How quickly can you find a needle in a haystack? How well can you work with the stereo playing, the dog barking, and someone tugging on your sleeve? And how well can you sort through a large amount of irrelevant information to find the single item that you need to solve the problem? The following series of distraction tests may give you a chance to find out.

Each of the tests in this group involves finding the location of items (figures, letters, or numbers) that are surrounded or obscured by an irrelevant background. George Washington University psychologist Dr. Stephen Karp intentionally designed the backgrounds to distract you from your task and thus increase the tests' difficulty.

The skills involved in these distraction tests center on the psychological concept of visual-field dependence and independence. The *field-dependent* person tends to take what has been called a spectator approach to tasks such as these. He or she is affected by all that is going on around the task, even though the surrounding context is irrelevant. Conversely, the *field-independent* person tends to use more exacting approaches to problem analysis, discarding the irrelevant and focusing on what is called for by the task.

Although each of these tests involves a distracting context, they differ in the relationship of the significant objects to their surroundings. Two of the tests ask you to locate a figure in a context of similar shapes and objects. Another test involves the seemingly simple process of crossing out certain letters as quickly as you can. And the fourth consists of elementary-level arithmetic problems arranged in a context of graffiti.

Before you begin, give yourself every advantage by removing (if you can) any distractions not intended as part of the tests. The times on these tests are very brief.

INSTRUCTIONS

In the Figure Recognition Test you will be presented with a series of 13 designs across the top of the page. Each of these designs is repeated once in the lower part of the page, along with several irrelevant designs. Your task is to locate each of the top designs among the designs on the lower part of the page and circle it. The correct design appears below exactly as it is above, not as a mirror image nor otherwise altered.

Give yourself one minute to complete the test. You must work quickly. When your time is up, stop your work and turn the page to find your score.

©Karp, S.A. (ed.), Kit of Selected Distractions Tests, *Brooklyn, New York: Cognitive Tests, 1962.*

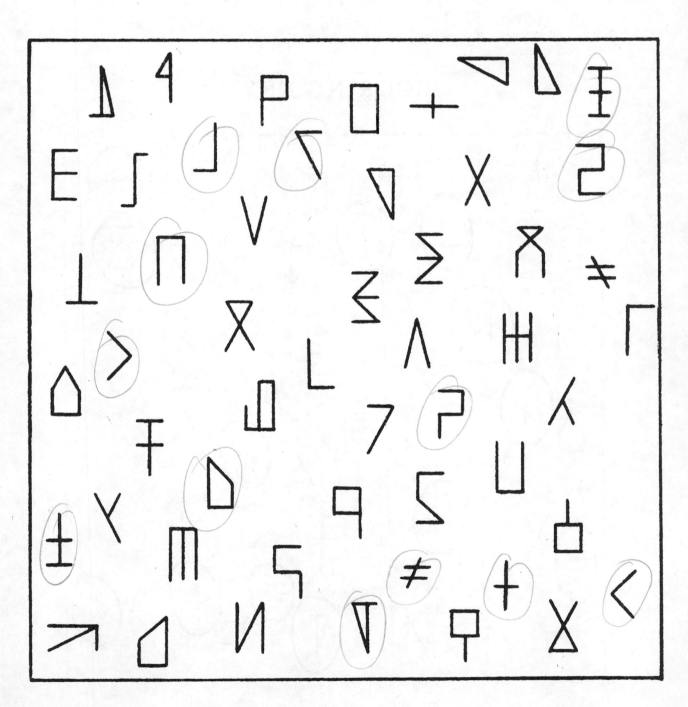

SCORING

To find your score, compare your responses on the test to those on the Scoring Key. Give yourself 1 point for each correct answer. There are 13 points possible. The norms for the test, defining strong, average, and weak performances, also appear on this page. Make a note of your score and go on to Tests 25, 26, and 27. At the end of Test 27 is an Interpretation section for the entire series of distraction tests.

TOTAL
SCORE 13

TEST NORMS

SCORING KEY

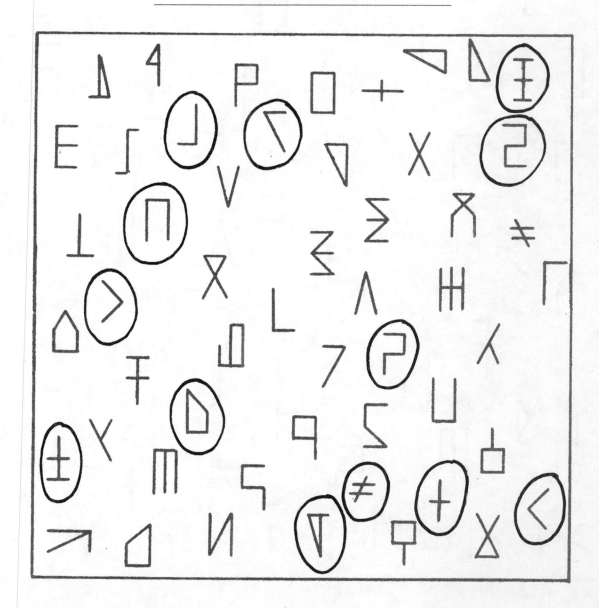

25. Cancellation Test

INSTRUCTIONS

In the Cancellation Test you will be presented with a sheet of randomly arranged letters, like those below.

pskdcmosgfyqwepkasidtogmqftshbdrpzvxqufsidiwg
hpigvjembsfgtcdbvmzkhfpolabgiflureqihpjoabkbt

Your task is to cross out the letters a, t, *and* c *every time you see them, starting with the top line and working your way down, line by line.*
  Give yourself five minutes to complete the test. When your time is up, stop your work and turn the page to find your score.

©*Karp, S.A. (ed.),* Kit of Selected Distractions Tests, *Brooklyn, New York: Cognitive Tests, 1962.*

hpigvjemvsfgtcdbvmzknfpolabgiflureqihpjoabkbt
ndefxkjcdtmwfzeojqlfhyeijqpzhkeqtvyziskfpvrjy
mxniufkfvxypralkjowqfvpystexralpbiqredjfuqzih
pskdcmosgfyqwepkasidtogmqftshbdrpzvxqufsidiwg
tohxwaklbvxzfiearlsyvqfuildtapqevkntouodszeyw
xfvozpkrqbeftkxivjybuacdsqbumehredxygjwhblftg
yekdwzdxppokwizyedgowacpkmjrhltolvdaxkhmwzfkm
ytejscqioxhtfayublrrezpwmslbjgevnxiwoybhazbsr
tndrbuclmtcazyjglvptvohswfzvqrhimajyozptqabam
mosfczubkijpcyfaoujmzcikrbxpfcndsoaljyrbcvdsg
ykmbfcgzjprinqksfgawulcrkgdfuikaczymdoxfqukzq
nwujgredlzupnjxgdfzemojndxciuzwbjqdghvudiqodu
zbucgtpqkuwljorbkspwujtoebnmwadvsnvkuvroljwlm
icuofmaedjxcgvnlsfjzbaruxnfmodhycvsqrukfdaiex
xmphfdogcietmoivicdnfhqjxgoasvyntxwbqpfhynduz
ekdzjrylqamsptkgzonieusyrpnqzcsvtuiygfkpzsnlt
vkpasynjkhopuywqzcljgyrovdwnmuqkfxihyvjlxsvjb
wlusnmxgbfyikpaugxltybingujsxyrpmhgvbzluxcena
wgtjfablhxnqsynazlegmsyqjdnxledztagmahfloqusy
rtmhlciqagnyrcltljhubrbmqepgicsvmrwxpcqztbaks
yvxgzodcabexmnfyutjrxnzhwbbipcoledxintmhwplsu
lyngdwrakivqyselwfikuhvxgdcimwopvqkinudwlmppb
htxvxysizcldqwpjuzraehwlvsrmyubevpniglqsnvzer
uyxnzanigzveqrpwosnltxyujwgakmehlcynbkpwvpzdl
oahylspktgemnqszejicodrhesbuhfmzopnqckegmunzd
xeakogjbeavupsrmxtqwkhbcoryuaghimzakwbnqjriat
ldevcbtqnwlxdrzyecgrpinajhxtqkyimuwegoklebamr
qrgnvjswhdexcormuplhqrnzetwblhefrtjamifhjcxre
blvzdnyheilabcfoneyhxatzowgnhyfnowbpxhtsdfvep
wimngsaectjqwhftypsogndeffkrpyikcnybkpwrselwd

167

SCORING

To find your score, count the number of *a*'s, *t*'s, and *c*'s that you crossed out. The Scoring Key shows the exact locations of the letters. There are 148 possible points. Note your score and compare your performance with the norms. Then go on to Test 26.

TOTAL
SCORE

TEST NORMS

CANCELLATION TEST NORMS

Strong performance:	115-148
Average performance:	90-114
Weak performance:	0-89

SCORING KEY

hpigvjemvsfg••dbvmzknfpol•bgiflureqihpjo•bkb•
ndefxkj•d•mwfzeojqlfhyeijqpzhkeq•vyziskfpvrjy
mxniufkfvxypr•lkjowqfvpys•exr•lpbiqredjfuqzih
pskd•mosgfyqwepk•sid•ogmqf•shbdrpzvxqufsidiwg
•ohxw•klbvxzfie•rlsyvqfuild••pqevkn•ouodszeyw
xfvozpkrqbef•kxivjybu••dsqbumehredxygjwhblf•g
yekdwzdxppokwizyedgow••pkmjrhl•olvd•xkhmwzfkm
y•ejs•qioxh•f•yubl•rezpwmslbjgevnxiwoybh•zbsr
•ndrbu•lm•••zyjglvp•vohswfzvqrhim•jyozp•q•b•m
mosf•zubkijp•yf•oujmz•ikrbxp••ndso•ljyrb•vdsg
ykmbf•gzjprinqksfg•wul•rkgdfuik••zymdoxfqukzq
nwujgredlzupnjxgdfzemojndx•iuzwbjqdghvudiqodu
zbu•g•pqkuwljorbkspwuj•oebnmw•dvsnvkuvroljwlm
i•uofm•edjx•gvnlsfjzb•ruxnfmodhy•vsqrukfd•iex
xmphfdog•ie•moivi•dnfhqjxgo•svyn•xwbqpfhynduz
ekdzjrylq•msp•kgzonieusyrpnqz•sv•uiygfkpzsnl•
vkp•synjkhopuywqz•ljgyrovdwnmuqkfxihyvjlxsvjb
wlusnmxgb•yikp•ugxl•ybingujsxyrpmhgvbzlux•en•
wg•jf•blhxnqsyn•zlegmsyqjdnxledz••gm•hfloqusy
r•mhl•iq•gnyr•l•ljhubrbmqepgi•svmrwxp•qz•b•ks
yvxgzod••bexmnfyu•jrxnzhwbbip•oledxin•mhwplsu
lyngdwr•kivqyselwfikuhvxgd•imwopvqkinudwlmppb
h•xvxysiz•ldqwpjuzr•ehwlvsrmyubevpniglqsnvzer
uyxnz•nigzveqrpwosnl•xyujwg•kmehl•ynbkpwvpzdl
o•hylspk•gemnqszeji•odrhesbuhfmzopnq•kegmunzd
xe•kogjbe•vupsrmx•qwkhb•oryu•ghimz•kwbnqjri••
ldev•b•qnwlxdrzye•grpin•jhx•qkyimuwegokleb•mr
qrgnvjswhdex•ormuplhqrnze•wblhefr•j•mifhj•xre
blvzdnyheil•b•foneyhx••zowgnhyfnowbpxh•sdfvep
wimngs•e••jqwhf•ypsogndeffkrpyik•nybkpwrselwd

26. Arithmetic Test

INSTRUCTIONS

In the Arithmetic Test, you will be given a series of 24 arithmetic problems, such as the following:

5−3+8=_____   7+2−9=_____   6+1+3=_____

All of the problems you will be given are at this level of difficulty. They are divided into 8 rows of 3 problems each. You are to write in the correct answer to all 24 problems as quickly as you can.

To make your task a little more difficult, the page on which the problems are presented has been filled with a lot of irrelevant material, such as pictures, words, and doodles. These have nothing to do with your task and have only been put there to distract you.

You will have only one minute in which to complete the test, so you will have to work quickly. When your time is up, stop your work and turn the page to score the test.

©Karp, S.A. (ed.), Kit of Selected Distractions Tests, Brooklyn, New York: Cognitive Tests, 1962.

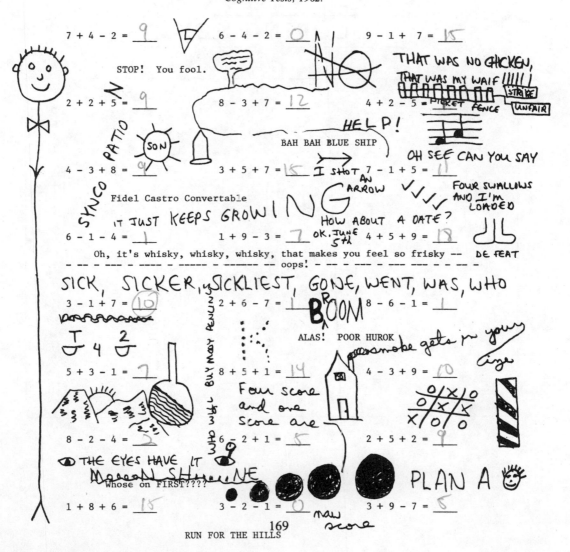

RUN FOR THE HILLS

SCORING

To find your score, compare your answers to those shown here. Give yourself 1 point for each question you answered correctly. Note your score and compare your performance to the norms. Then go on to the last test in this series, Test 27.

23

TOTAL SCORE

TEST NORMS

ARITHMETIC TEST NORMS

Strong performance:	22-24
Average performance:	15-21
Weak performance:	0-14

SCORING KEY

9	0	15
9	12	1
9	15	11
1	7	18
9	1	1
7	14	10
2	5	9
15	0	5

27. Embedded Figures Test

INSTRUCTIONS

In the Embedded Figures Test, you will be presented with 16 simple figures, each followed by 2 complex designs. The simple figure has been hidden in both of the complex designs to its right. Your task is to find the simple hidden figure and circle it in both complex designs.

As in the example above, the hidden figure is always upright and always the same size as at left. It appears only once in each of the complex designs next to it. If one design puzzles you, go on to the next one, and come back to the difficult one later.

Give yourself one minute in which to complete this test. You will have to work quickly. When your time is up, stop your work and turn the page to score the test.

©Karp, S.A. (ed.), Kit of Selected Distractions Tests, *Brooklyn, New York: Cognitive Tests, 1962.*

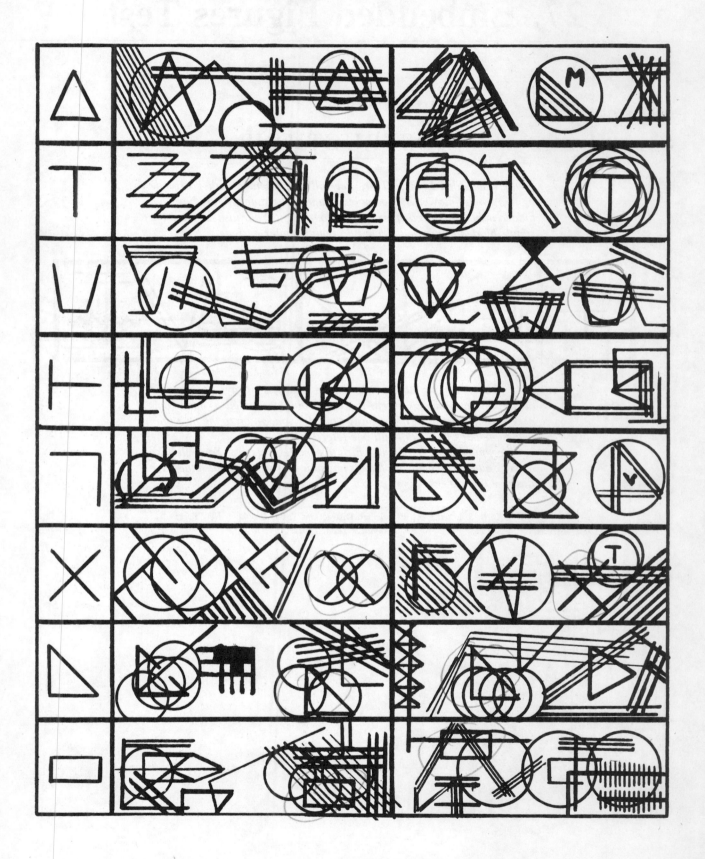

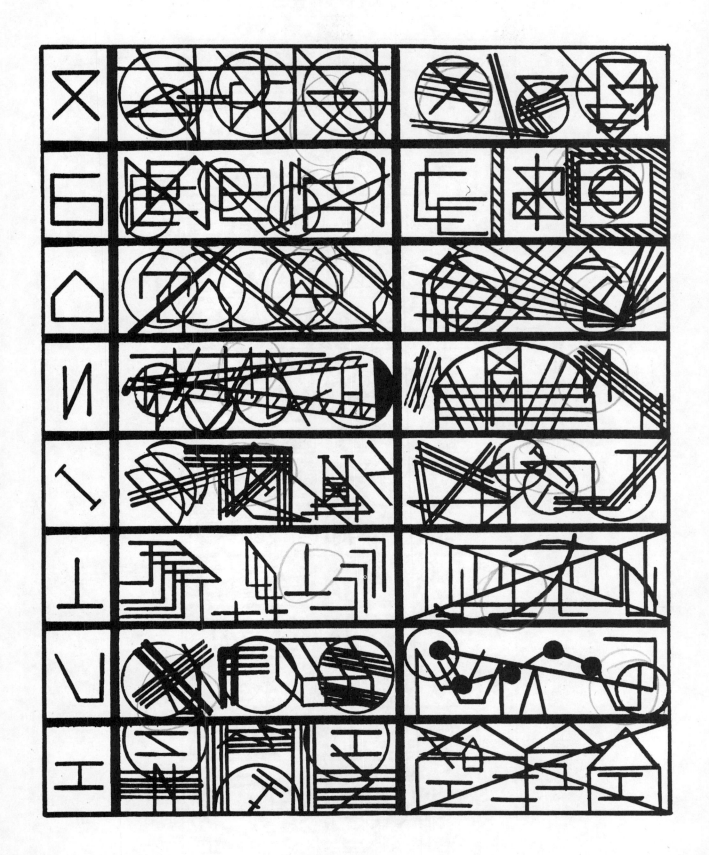

SCORING KEY

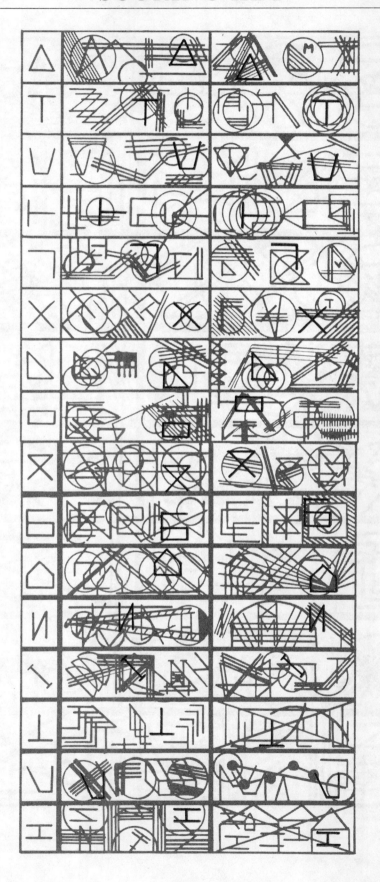

SCORING

To find your score, count the number of hidden figures you have located. There are 32 possible points. If you are not sure of the location of the hidden figures, you may wish to refer to the Scoring Key. Note your score and compare your performance to the norms below.

TOTAL SCORE

TEST NORMS

EMBEDDED FIGURES TEST NORMS

Strong performance:	26-32
Average performance:	19-25
Weak performance:	0-18

INTERPRETATION

The four distraction tests measure similar skills. To help you interpret your scores, you may wish to record them in the spaces below.

Psychological research has shown that the specific skills involved in field independence and distracting-context tasks are related to a number of personality characteristics. As testing expert Dr. Anne Anastasi wrote in 1982, "The scope and diversity of research on field independence is truly impressive, ranging from interpersonal relations to learning and memory, mathematics achievement and cross-cultural differences."

The research suggests that people who score high on tests such as these distraction tests (field-independent people) tend to take an active, participant approach to learning and problem solving. Those who score mostly low (field-dependent people) are more likely to take the spectator approach to such situations, waiting for others to provide cues as to the best steps to take. But low scorers also seem to pay more attention to social cues and thus are often responsive to the behavior of others.

High scorers are likely to find their skills useful in leadership or program development positions, jobs that require quick decision making and rapid data analysis. Those who score lower may be more comfortable and successful in positions that place a premium on a slow, methodical approach to problems. They may prefer working out solutions with other people.

An average or weak performance can be positive if you are aware of your strengths and needs, and use them effectively in planning your career. As Dr. Anastasi also noted, "It appears that neither end of the field-dependent—field-independent continuum is necessarily favorable or unfavorable; rather, the value of deviations in either direction depends on the demands of particular situations."

TEST 24 FIGURE RECOGNITION	TEST 25 CANCELLATION	TEST 26 ARITHMETIC	TEST 27 EMBEDDED FIGURES
☑ Strong	☑ Strong	☑ Strong	☑ Strong
☐ Average	☐ Average	☐ Average	☐ Average
☐ Weak	☐ Weak	☐ Weak	☐ Weak